Harwood Fundamentals of Pure and Applied Economics

MARKET STRUCTURE AND TECHNOLOGICAL CHANGE

Routledge
Taylor & Francis Group
LONDON AND NEW YORK

FUNDAMENTALS OF PURE AND APPLIED ECONOMICS

ECONOMICS OF TECHNOLOGICAL CHANGE II
In 2 Volumes

MARKET STRUCTURE AND TECHNOLOGICAL CHANGE

WILLIAM L BALDWIN
AND JOHN T SCOTT

Routledge
Taylor & Francis Group
LONDON AND NEW YORK

First published in 1987 by
Harwood Academic Publishers GmbH

Published in 2001 by
Routledge
2 Park Square, Milton Park, Abingdon, Oxfordshire OX14 4RN
711 Third Avenue, New York, NY 10017

First issued in paperback 2014

Routledge is an imprint of the Taylor and Francis Group, an informa company

British Library Cataloguing in Publication Data
A CIP catalogue record for this book
is available from the British Library

Market Structure and Technological Change

Economics of Technological Change II: 2 Volumes

Harwood Fundamentals of Pure & Applied Economics
ISBN 978-0-415-26933-9 (hbk)
ISBN 978-0-415-75368-5 (pbk)

Market Structure and Technological Change

William L. Baldwin

and

John T. Scott
Dartmouth College, USA

A volume in the Economics of Technological Change section
edited by

F. M. Scherer
Harvard University, USA

harwood academic publishers
chur · london · paris · new york · melbourne

Published 1987
Second Printing 1991

Harwood Academic Publishers

Post Office Box 197
London WC2E 9PX
United Kingdom

58, rue Lhomond
75005 Paris
France

Post Office Box 786
Cooper Station
New York, New York 10276
United States of America

Private Bag 8
Camberwell, Victoria 3124
Australia

Library of Congress Cataloging-in-Publication Data

Baldwin, William L., 1928–
Market structure and technological change.

(Fundamentals of pure and applied economics; vol. 17.
Economics of technological change section, ISSN 0191-1708)
Bibliography: p.
Includes index
1. Industrial organization (Economic theory)
2. Technological innovations—Economic aspects.
I. Scott, John T., 1947– II. Title. III. Series:
Fundamentals of pure and applied economics; vol. 17.
IV. Series: Fundamentals of pure and applied economics.
Economics of technological change section.
HD2326.B35 1987 338′.06 86-25780
ISBN 3-7186-0375-6

Contents

Introduction to the Series

Drawing on a personal network, an economist can still relatively easily stay well informed in the narrow field in which he works, but to keep up with the development of economics as a whole is a much more formidable challenge. Economists are confronted with difficulties associated with the rapid development of their discipline. There is a risk of "balkanization" in economics, which may not be favorable to its development.

Fundamentals of Pure and Applied Economics has been created to meet this problem. The discipline of economics has been subdivided into sections (listed at the back of this volume). These sections include short books, each surveying the state of the art in a given area.

Each book starts with the basic elements and goes as far as the most advanced results. Each should be useful to professors needing material for lectures, to graduate students looking for a global view of a particular subject, to professional economists wishing to keep up with the development of their science, and to researchers seeking convenient information on questions that incidentally appear in their work.

Each book is thus a presentation of the state of the art in a particular field rather than a step-by-step analysis of the development of the literature. Each is a high-level presentation but accessible to anyone with a solid background in economics, whether engaged in business, government, international organizations, teaching, or research in related fields.

Three aspects of *Fundamentals of Pure and Applied Economics* should be emphasized:

—First, the project covers the whole field of economics, not only theoretical or mathematical economics.

—Second, the project is open-ended and the number of books is not predetermined. If new interesting areas appear, they will generate additional books.
—Last, all the books making up each section will later be grouped to constitute one or several volumes of an Encyclopedia of Economics.

The editors of the sections are outstanding economists who have selected as authors for the series some of the finest specialists in the world.

J. Lesourne *H. Sonnenschein*

Market Structure and Technological Change

WILLIAM L. BALDWIN and JOHN T. SCOTT

Dartmouth College, USA

1. THE SCHUMPETERIAN LEGACY

Any systematic treatment of the literature on the relationship between the organization of industry and technological progress must begin with the pioneering work of Joseph A. Schumpeter. Subsequent studies, theoretical and empirical alike, often identify their topic as yet another contribution to the "Schumpeterian" hypothesis, model, or system. Given the fundamental role of Schumpeter's thought and the fragmentary portions of his system examined by various subsequent writers, a brief review of his vision and analysis of the interactions among innovation, market structure, and economic progress seems a necessary prologue.[1]

Schumpeter's view of the process of innovation in a modern, imperfectly competitive economy is most forcefully expressed in three chapters of his 1942 book, *Capitalism, Socialism, and Democracy* [283]; and this work is the most frequently cited source of the "Schumpeterian hypothesis." Schumpeter challenged the conventional wisdom regarding monopoly and competition when he

[1] The distinction between vision and analysis was crucial to Schumpeter's own thought and to his assessment of other economists' contributions. He wrote, [285, p. 41], "Obviously, in order to be able to posit to ourselves any problems at all, we should first have to visualize a distinct set of coherent phenomena as a worth-while object of our analytical methods. In other words, analytic effort is of necessity preceded by a preanalytic cognitive act that supplies the raw material for the analytic effort. In this book, this preanalytic cognitive act will be called Vision."

asserted that:

> As soon as we go into details and inquire into the individual items in which progress was most conspicuous, the trail leads not to the doors of those firms that work under conditions of comparatively free competition but precisely to the doors of the large concerns . . . and a shocking suspicion dawns upon us that big business may have had more to do with creating that standard of life than with keeping it down. [p. 82].
> [T]he large scale establishment or unit of control . . . has come to be the most powerful engine of . . . progress and in particular of the long-run expansion of total output not only in spite of, but to a considerable extent through . . . strategy which looks so restrictive when viewed in the individual case and from the individual point of time. In this respect, perfect competition is . . . inferior, and has no title to being set up as a model of ideal efficiency. [p. 106].

Schumpeter's argument is that "the kind of competition which counts" [p. 84] in a modern industrialized economy is most effectively engaged in by "the large scale establishment or unit of control" that does not "work under conditions of comparatively free competition." There are two distinctly different elements to this hypothesis—a causal relationship between size of firm and innovation, and one between a firm's market power and its innovative activities. Schumpeter did not distinguish clearly between the two. Rather, he regarded size and market power as inextricably linked in modern capitalist reality, at least to the extent that the primary sources of innovation are involved. This can be seen most readily in his earlier works. In *Business Cycles* [282], for example, he noted, "But 'monopoly' really means any large-scale business. And since economic 'progress' in this country is largely the result of work done within a number of concerns at no time much greater than 300 or 400, any serious threat to the functioning of these will spread paralysis in the economic organism." [p. 1044].

In *Capitalism, Socialism, and Democracy,* Schumpeter did not spell out the significance he attributed to sheer size in the ability of the modern firm to innovate. Perhaps he thought this relationship, as integral as it is to his vision of modern capitalist economic development, is too obvious to require analysis. He did, however, analyze the manner in which market power promotes innovation. The essence of Schumpeter's argument is that innovation is an activity fraught with uncertainty, and that large-scale innovation may not be attractive unless some sort of "insurance" is available to the potential entrepreneur. Noting that if "a war risk is insurable, nobody objects to a firm's collecting the cost of this insurance from the buyers of its products," Schumpeter argued that by analogy a firm unable to obtain insurance against the failure of an innovation should be able to engage in "a price strategy aiming at the same end." [p. 88]. Thus, monopolistic power in existing product markets may be a precondition for innovation. Further, anticipated market power in new products may provide essential incentives to innovate, since "enterprise would in most cases be impossible if it were not known from the outset that exceptionally favorable situations are likely to arise," the exploitation of which "requires strategy that in the short run is often restrictive." [pp. 89–90].

In Schumpeter's view, "competition from the new commodity, the new technology, the new source of supply, the new type of organization," was so much more effective than traditional price competition that "it becomes a matter of comparative indifference whether competition in the ordinary sense functions more or less promptly." [283, pp. 84–5]. Further:

> A system . . . that at *every* given point of time fully utilizes its possibilities to the best advantage may yet in the long run be inferior to a system that does so at *no* given point of time, because the latter's failure to do so may be a condition for the level or speed of long-run performance. [283, p. 83. Italics in original].

In her introduction to *History of Economic Analysis* [285], Elizabeth Boody Schumpeter noted that "After herculean labor, J.A.S. had finished his monumental *Business Cycles* in 1938 and sought relaxation in *Capitalism, Socialism, and Democracy,* which he regarded as distinctly a 'popular' offering that he expected to finish in a few months." [p. v.]. As a "popular" work, *Capitalism, Socialism, and Democracy* is intentionally long on vision, and sparing on analysis. To place *Capitalism, Socialism, and Democracy* in its proper perspective, one must recognize that, to a far greater extent than most economists whose scholarly contributions have extended over several decades, Schumpeter's later works expanded and elaborated on his earlier ones to construct a coherent system with the whole forming a consistent body of thought. (For a thoughtful, integrative exposition of this system, see [39]).

Although Schumpeter did introduce the concept of "creative destruction" in *Capitalism, Socialism, and Democracy,* and noted that competition from innovation "strikes not at the margins of the profits and the outputs of the existing firms but at their foundations and their very lives" [p. 84], he put stress on a short-term relationship in which characteristics of industrial structure were viewed as determinants of innovation. But in his earlier, more analytical work, Schumpeter had concentrated on a longer-term relationship in which the predominant feature is the effect of innovation and its diffusion on industrial structure.

Throughout, Schumpeter distinguished carefully between economic development and economic growth. The latter had been recognized by the classical economists as stemming from population growth and capital accumulation. But Schumpeter was critical of leading economists, including Smith, Mill, Walras, and Marshall, for their failure to incorporate innovation in their formal analyses. "Obviously," he noted, "the face of the earth would look very different if people . . . had done nothing else except multiply and save." Rather, economic development had stemmed from new methods of production and commerce. "This historic and irreversible change in the way of doing things we call 'innovation' and we define: innovations are changes in production functions which cannot be decomposed into infinitesimal steps. Add as many mail-coaches as you please, you will never get a railroad by so doing." [284, pp. 149–59, at p. 152]. Economic development, then, necessarily impacted on industrial structure. As he noted in *Business Cycles,* "Capitalism is essentially a process of (endogenous) economic change. Without that change or, more precisely, that kind of change we have called evolution, capitalist society cannot exist . . . ." [282, p. 1033. Parenthesis as in original]. This "endogenous" and "evolutionary" feature of the larger Schumpeterian system has been recognized by a few subsequent modelers, and indeed forms the core of their analyses.

2. RIVALRY AND THE OPTIMALITY OF INNOVATIVE INVESTMENT

2.1. Measuring the benefits of innovation, with initial insights about how market structure affects the generation of those benefits

The Schumpeterian legacy has fostered exploration of the links between innovative performance and market structure. Market structure encompasses economically important features of the business environment including the number and size distribution (concentration) of a market's sellers, barriers to entry, firms' sizes, and diversification. The literature reviewed here seeks to explain how innovations generate social and private benefits in alternative market structures ranging from monopoly to pure competition. Market structure affects the generation of those benefits, because it affects firms' perceptions of the private benefits and costs of innovation. The purposeful behavior of firms seeking gain then varies with market structure. When social and private benefits and costs diverge, the innovative investment in a market will not typically be optimal.

Throughout, research and development (R & D) means firms' activities directed at the creation of innovations which may be introduced by bringing either new products to market or new processes into production. The benefits flowing from research are the values net of opportunity costs of new products and new processes. Mansfield *et al.* [186] extend concepts and models used by Griliches [95] and Arrow [7] to define the net benefit of such innovations as the gain in economic surplus. The analysis focuses on three cases—new processes used by the innovating firms, new products sold by the innovator to firms that use the products in their production processes, and new products used by households. In all three cases, the net gain to society is the gain in total surplus. Figure 1 shows the demand curve, $\mathbf{DD'}$, for a final product and its price, $\mathbf{P_1}$, and quantity, $\mathbf{Q_1}$, before an innovation which reduces the social costs of its production. After the innovation, constant unit social cost is $\mathbf{C_2}$, and the quantity and (supra-competitive) price are $\mathbf{Q_2}$ and $\mathbf{P_2}$ respectively.

If the difference between revenues and costs were nil before the innovation, and if all the social costs of innovative investment are included in the constant unit cost $\mathbf{C_2}$, then the net social benefit of the innovation is given by the area $\mathbf{P_1ABEC_2}$. Mansfield *et al.* [186] develop the concepts and detailed analysis needed to make this general model operational for each of the three cases they explore.

As Nelson and Winter [219] have observed, using a diagram suggested by Levin [219, p. 116, footnote 4] and reproduced in Figure 2, in a dynamic, progressive, concentrated industry, market structure will affect not only the extent of the deadweight loss

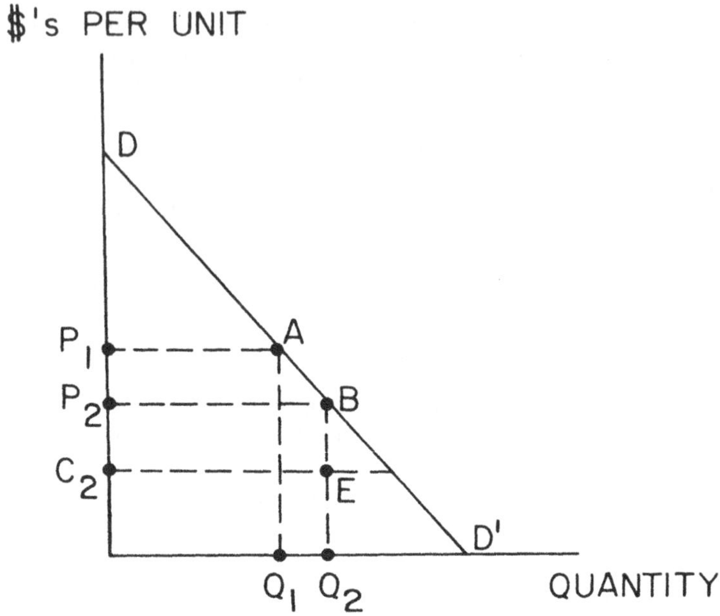

FIGURE 1

traditionally associated with market power. Additionally, the divergence of the best-practice technology from the potential best and the divergence of average practice from best practice will be affected. In Figure 2, **C** denotes the unit costs for the potential best technology given efficient research; actual-practice unit costs range from $\hat{c}$ to $\hat{c}'$; price is **P′** and output is **Q′**. Then one way to characterize the Schumpeterian question is to ask how market structure affects the cost that arises because best practice diverges from the potential best (area **ĉEBC**), the cost stemming from divergence between average and best practice (area **ĉĉ′F**), and the deadweight loss (area **AEF**) that results because too few resources are allocated to production in an industry where the firms have market power. Potential surplus—area **DBC**—exceeds actual surplus—area **DAĉ′ĉ**—by these three types of costs, and their size and significance (as well as their distribution) will vary with market structure.

As Mansfield *et al.* [186, p. 240, footnote 29] observe, the models

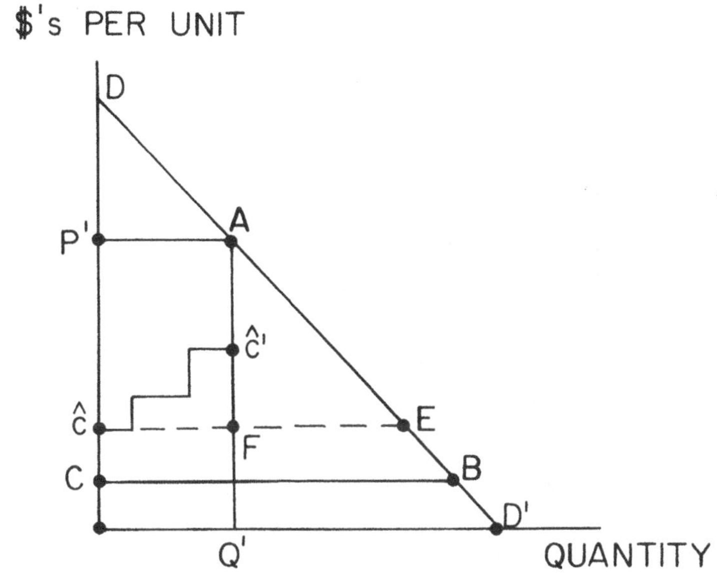

FIGURE 2

they develop are not applicable if the innovation's effects cannot be interpreted as a reduction in social costs. Lancaster's [139] approach allows conceptualization of new consumer products that are in the same general class as a set of existing products. Products provide a bundle of characteristics, each product being characterized by the fixed proportion in which those characteristics are provided. For expositional purposes, consider the class of products providing various amounts of characteristics $\mathbf{Z}_1$ and $\mathbf{Z}_2$. Figure 3 shows two such products, **A** and **B**. Product **A** provides two units of $\mathbf{Z}_2$ for each unit of $\mathbf{Z}_1$, while product **B** provides one unit of $\mathbf{Z}_2$ for each unit of $\mathbf{Z}_1$. (Mixing of products is assumed not possible, otherwise two goods, corresponding to the vertical and horizontal axes, would suffice to generate the entire set of products.)

In this framework, process innovation allows a given resource outlay to produce a combination of $\mathbf{Z}_1$ and $\mathbf{Z}_2$ farther out along a given ray from the origin. A product innovation creates new rays. Lancaster uses this framework to ask whether, given technologies and preferences, the economy will generate too many rays. For the

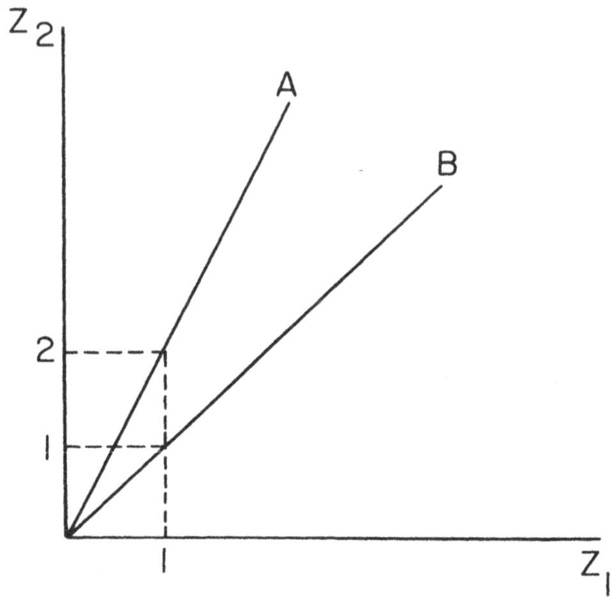

FIGURE 3

problem of research performance, the issue is whether the cost of a given innovation is justified by the benefits of the innovation, allowing movement out along an existing ray or making feasible a new ray.

More generally, one needs to ask if the innovation establishing a new ray allows attainment of the same level of utility with fewer resources, including the cost of innovation. Our issue is whether market structure optimally guides investment in new products. Scherer [267] has developed this problem by working with the economic surplus function over product attribute space for a given class of products.

Scherer measures the continuum of rays with a continuum of points on a line—the attribute-measure line. Consumers have preferences indicating their most desired combinations of product characteristics, and hence, their most desired ray in Lancastrian space or point on the attribute-measure line. Consumers with their different preferences are assumed to have equal incomes and to be uniformly distributed along the attribute line. Figure 4 shows the

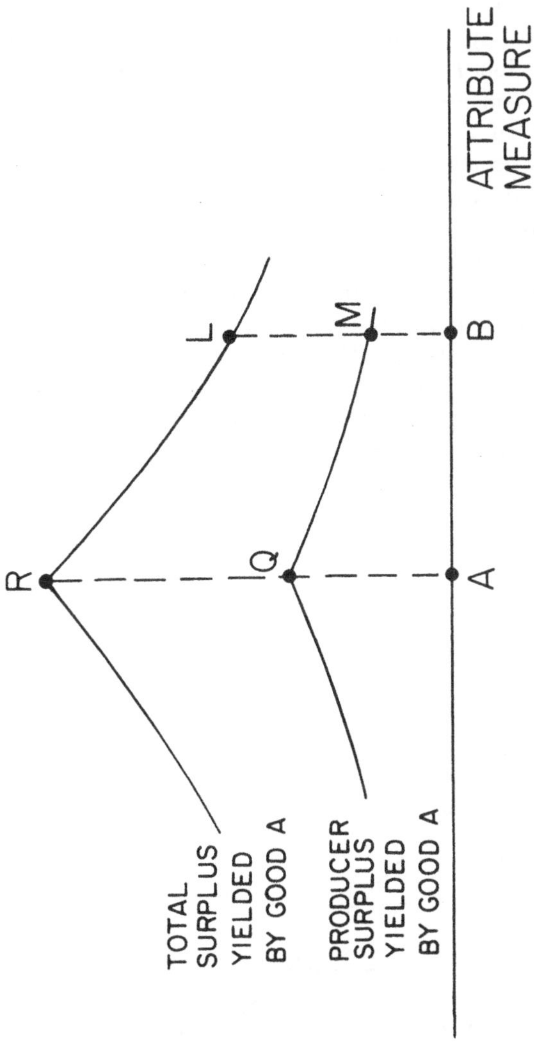
TOTAL SURPLUS YIELDED BY GOOD A
PRODUCER SURPLUS YIELDED BY GOOD A
R
Q
L
M
A
B
ATTRIBUTE MEASURE

FIGURE 4

producers' surplus, measured by line segment $\overline{\mathbf{QA}}$ (where the overbar denotes a line segment), and the consumers' surplus $\overline{\mathbf{RQ}}$ from production and sale, to consumers located at **A**, of the good described by ray **A** in Figure 3. For consumers whose most preferred product is **B**, producers' surplus from the sale of good **A** is $\overline{\mathbf{MB}}$; while consumers' surplus is $\overline{\mathbf{LM}}$.

The shape of the surplus functions over the product attribute space follows because consumers whose most preferred product is **B** will buy less of **A** at a given price than will consumers whose most preferred product is **A**. Figure 5 shows these producer and consumer surpluses in the context of demand, $\mathbf{D_AD'_A}$, for good **A** by consumers whose most preferred good is **A**; demand $\mathbf{D_BD'_B}$ for good **A** by consumers whose most preferred good is **B**; and constant unit production costs, **C**. The correspondence between Figures 4 and 5 is as follows. The consumers' surplus generated by sales of **A** to consumers with preferences located at **A** is the line segment $\overline{\mathbf{RQ}}$ in Figure 4. The amount $\overline{\mathbf{RQ}}$ equals the area $\mathbf{D_ASP}$ in Figure 5. The producers' surplus is measured by $\overline{\mathbf{QA}}$ in Figure 4, or, equivalently,

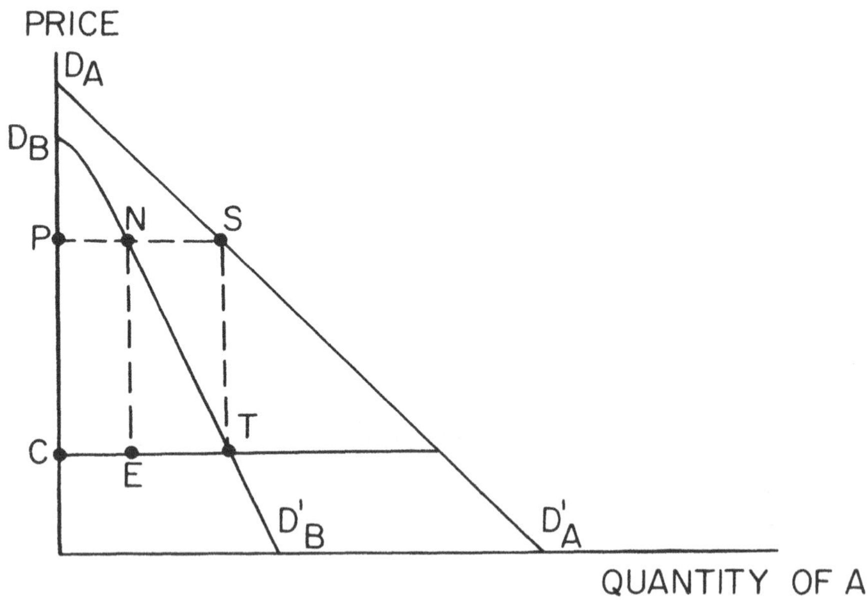

FIGURE 5

area **PSTC** in Figure 5. Similarly, $\overline{\mathbf{LM}}$ in Figure 4, indicates the same consumer surplus as the area **$\mathbf{D_B}$NP** in Figure 5; while $\overline{\mathbf{MB}}$ and **PNEC** reflect an identical amount of producer surplus.

Now the problem of market structure here is that the innovating firm compares its cost of innovative investment with *its* own gain in producer's surplus, while the social planner would compare the social cost of innovative investment with the net gain in total surplus. Introducing a new product creates new surplus functions as some consumers shift consumption from old products to the new ones. New consumer surplus would be considered a benefit by society but not by the innovating firm. Surplus shifted (cannibalized) from consumers or other firms to the innovator would be considered a gain by the innovating firm but not by society. Scherer explains that for a new product that is a close substitute for existing products, new consumers' surplus and new producers' surplus are relatively small, while cannibalized surplus will be relatively high. Hence, we could anticipate circumstances in which markets would generate too much product innovation.

In Figure 6, the shaded area is the new surplus which the social planner would weigh against the cost (not explicitly shown) of innovating the new product **B**, given that products **A** and **C** existed previously. But the innovating firm would consider only its gain in producer surplus. If a new firm (i.e., a firm other than the one or ones producing goods **A** and **C**) introduced the good **B**, it would weigh the striped area against the innovation cost (not explicitly shown). When good **B** is a close substitute for goods **A** and **C**, the striped area will be large relative to the shaded area. In such circumstances, markets open to nonprice competition might be expected to generate too much innovative investment. Using Figure 6 and varying the relative sizes of the striped and shaded areas and the innovation cost, various cases can be adduced.

2.2. The stark dichotomy of monopoly versus competition

Schumpeter's sweeping vision posed a challenge for theorists who have examined implications for technological performance of such structural features as firms' sizes and diversification, markets' concentration, and barriers to entry, along with concomitant degrees of market power. Early analyses tended to compare the

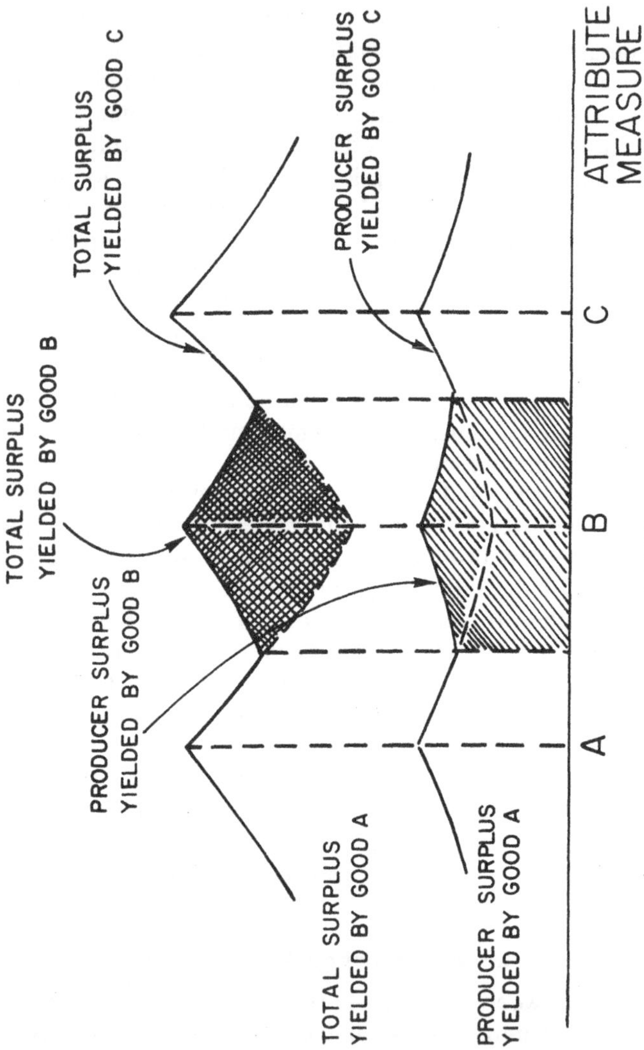
TOTAL SURPLUS YIELDED BY GOOD A
PRODUCER SURPLUS YIELDED BY GOOD A
PRODUCER SURPLUS YIELDED BY GOOD B
TOTAL SURPLUS YIELDED BY GOOD B
TOTAL SURPLUS YIELDED BY GOOD C
PRODUCER SURPLUS YIELDED BY GOOD C
A
B
C
ATTRIBUTE MEASURE

FIGURE 6

extremes of monopoly and competition, while much recent work extends those analyses into intermediate (albeit highly stylized) structures.

Bain [8, pp. 226–31, 325, 347, 451–52] provided an early assessment that is in accord with much of the later conventional wisdom. It can be characterized as follows. If markets are to provide rewards to innovators, the expectation of rents in the post-innovation market is a crucial incentive. Of course these rents may be the quasi-rents obtained in a gradually adjusting competitive market. Those returns would be smaller than what the monopolist would receive, *ceteris paribus,* but might nonetheless provide sufficient inducement for innovative investment. To the extent that innovation comes from established firms that anticipate subsequent imitation and substitutable innovations from competitors, a less competitive market structure before innovation occurs would lead to the expectation of less competition and higher returns in the post-innovation market. Further, monopoly protected by entry barriers, and to some extent [8, p. 231, p. 325, and p. 347] more concentrated industry structures, would provide supranormal profits and hence internal financing for innovative investment.

On the other hand, according to Bain and Salter [258, pp. 92–93], highly concentrated market structures protected from entry may have poor innovative performance if the close-knit group is content with its old monopoly position and feels no competitive pressure to replace it with a new one. Also, as Swan [299, 300] and White [328, chapters 11 and 14; 329] have explained, product innovations that are imperfect substitutes for the product offered by a monopolist may appear profitable to new competitors while being unprofitable to the monopolist if the innovation merely cannibalizes the latter's own existing profits.[2] Further, from Bain [8, p. 227], Brozen [31], Fellner [65], and Salter [258, p. 92], competition may increase the speed with which new process innovations are introduced under the following conditions: (1) if the new average total cost is greater than the average variable costs for the old technique, (2) if the increase in equilibrium output is greater for the competitive case than for the monopoly case, and (3) if a new plant adds less output

[2] On the other hand, new products complementary to existing ones will be particularly attractive to a monopolist. See Ben-Zion and Fixler [17].

than the increase needed to restore equilibrium in the competitive case but more than needed in the monopoly case. This is so because, in the absence of strategic behavior or significant output expansion, incumbents, whether monopolists or not, will replace old facilities only when the average total cost with the new technique is less than the existing plant's average variable cost.

Arrow [7] also addressed the issue of market structure and technological change by comparing pure monopoly with pure competition. His analysis spawned a large literature. Arrow posited a monopolist of R & D activity—that is, there is no competition in either the pre- or post-innovation market for the invention. This monopolist inventor, protected completely from competition in the R & D activity, either licenses the cost-reducing invention to a competitive industry or, in the case where he also monopolizes the product market, uses the invention himself. Arrow reasoned that the product-market monopolist's incentive to invent is the difference between post-innovation profits and pre-innovation profits, while the monopolistic inventor setting a royalty rate for a competitive industry has an incentive equal to his royalties.

In the "drastic" case, where the post-innovation monopoly price is less than the pre-innovation competitive price, the incentive to invent is clearly greater for the inventor selling the rights to use the invention to a competitive industry than it is for a product-market monopolist facing the same demand curve. This result is reached since the inventor selling the rights can set a royalty rate such that the post-innovation price is at the new monopoly level; and with competition among the producers, the royalties received will equal that entire monopoly profit. The product-market monopolist, however, must calculate its net profit from introducing the innovation as the post-innovation profit minus the pre-innovation profit it obtained from its monopoly.

Referring to Figure 7, in the somewhat more complicated case where the invention is not drastic, and the post-innovation price in the case where the product market is monopolized, $\mathbf{P_{m2}}$, exceeds the pre-innovation cost, $\mathbf{C_1}$, the product-market monopolist's incentive is the change in revenue, $\mathbf{AEQ_{m2}Q_{m1}}$, less the change in production costs, $\mathbf{BEQ_{m2}Q_{m1} - P_cABC}$. Because of diminishing marginal revenue, that incentive, $\mathbf{P_cABC + ABE}$, is less than $\mathbf{P_cFEC}$, which is the royalty rate, $\mathbf{P_cC}$, the inventor could charge,

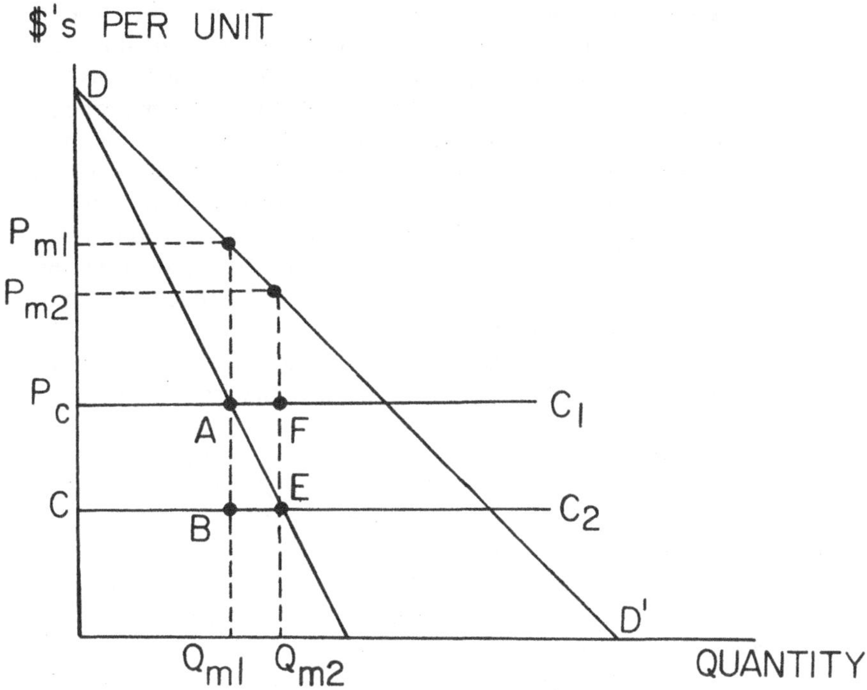

FIGURE 7

given competition, multiplied by the monopoly post-innovation output, $\mathbf{Q_{m2}}$. *A fortiori,* the product-market monopolist exploiting his own nondrastic invention obtains less than the royalties available to an inventor licensing the technology to a competitive industry, on the entire competitive output, which in this case must exceed the post-innovation monopoly output [7]. In sum, a fixed amount of R & D costs (not explicitly shown) must be overcome, and the rewards are more likely to be enough when the cost-reducing invention is used in a competitive industry.

Although in Arrow's formulation, the incentive for either drastic or nondrastic innovation is greatest for the case of a competitive industry, subsequent work [58, 340, 119, 222, 223, 109, 53, 54, 326, 69, 59, 164] makes clear that whether innovation is more or less likely depends on factors from which Arrow abstracted, even restricting the contrasted structural conditions for the industry using the invention to monopoly and competition. For example, Waterson [326] reconsiders the question raised by Arrow, but does not characterize innovation as a general reduction in unit cost. Instead the "inventor" monopolizes a new input. Whereas the monopolist user of the input gets the input at marginal cost, in pricing the new input for competitive users the input monopolist induces factor substitution on the part of the competitive users, so that Arrow's general inferences regarding relative incentives need not follow.

Fixler [69] preserves Arrow's general unit cost reduction but introduces bilateral monopoly between an independent inventor and the monopolized product market on the one hand, or the competitive industry (represented by a trade association) on the other. Arrow's original formulation avoided the issue of bilateral monopoly, since in the case where the using industry was a monopoly, the inventor was that monopolist [340]. Fixler also introduces risk, with a given level of research yielding an uncertain reduction in unit costs. He considers the inventor's attitude toward risk by making the expected utility of profit the inventor's objective function and then contrasting behavior when the inventor is risk-neutral (the utility function is linear) with behavior given risk aversion (utility increases with profits, but at a decreasing rate). He follows earlier modifications [58] of Arrow's approach by equalizing the pre-innovation outputs of the competitive and monopoly industries being compared. But in contrast, he follows Arrow's original assumption that the market demand curves are identical in the two alternative cases. He posits a great enough cost advantage in production for the monopolist to just offset its restriction of output. He can then show that whether the inventor or the industry dominates the bargaining process, and whether there is certainty or uncertainty, the relative strength of incentives to invent for competition versus monopoly is indeterminate. He demonstrates that the constraint of equal pre-innovation output levels for the monopolized and competitive industries causes the indeterminism. Removing the cost disadvantage of the competitive industry restores Arrow's original conclusion that the incentive to invent is greatest in the case of a competitive industry.

Donnenfeld [59] examines R & D when the demand for a monopolist's product is uncertain. He shows the risk-averse monopolist produces less output and undertakes less cost-reducing R & D than would be the case with certainty if the cost-reducing effect of R & D implies that the marginal cost of production, up to and including the equilibrium, falls as R & D increases (this case includes the simple reduction in constant unit cost explored by Arrow [7], Dasgupta and Stiglitz [49], and others). However, demand uncertainty can result in more cost-reducing R & D than the amount chosen with certain demand. That can occur when the new technologies available from R & D are especially efficient at lower outputs and inefficient at higher outputs. Since uncertainty in demand implies lower output, it can be desirable to spend more on R & D to obtain a technology that is efficient at low outputs. Donnenfeld develops the analogous result for the impact of an increase in uncertainty in the form of a mean-preserving spread of the distribution for demand.

In their review of the literature developing Arrow's model, Kamien and Schwartz [131, pp. 36–47] generalize the model by allowing the industry using the innovation to have **n** firms and a Cournot equilibrium for price and output. They then assume that the inventor guarantees the using industry its previous level of profits but no more, collecting payment with an optimal combination of a license fee and royalty charges—the royalty charges to induce output adjustments and the license fee to extract profits in excess of those earned on pre-innovation output. Under those conditions, the inventor receives a reward that increases with the competitiveness of the industry. Their formulation, like Arrow's, leaves open the possibility that bilateral bargaining strategies between the using industry and the "inventor" could affect innovative performance [131, p. 45].

These extensions of Arrow [7] compare special and restrictive cases of monopoly and competition. Many other Schumpeterian arguments imply important counterforces to the effects deduced in such narrowly focused models. Schumpeterian arguments in favor of large firm sizes imply that, for a given industry, the incentive to innovate will, *ceteris paribus*, be greater as sales are more concentrated under the control of a leading firm or group of firms. Of course, there can be large firms in unconcentrated industries. In any case, if not overcome by bureaucratic lethargy, large firms may be more efficient innovators because of scale economies in R & D, the greater value of R & D output for a large firm with well-developed marketing channels, and larger output over which to realize the benefits of process innovations.

Once diversification is introduced into Arrow-type models, the size issue is less clearly associated with increasing concentration. R & D is risky and costly, and the large firm can maintain a diversified portfolio of R & D projects. Arrow [7, p. 616] emphasizes that the devices for shifting risk are limited and imperfect. The rewards needed to induce innovation could be lessened if the firm could insure against its failure to develop a new product or process. But external insurance is not available; and thus if the corporation wants to insure itself, it must undertake many projects, each small relative to the company's size. Of course, if investors could diversify costlessly and if bankruptcy costs were nil, only the management would care about such insurance. However, even if those conditions obtain, there may be real advantages from diversification. Discussing basic research, Nelson [207, p. 302] emphasizes that the firm more diversified into several product markets is more likely to be able to appropriate research benefits in a post-innovation market, since it can more readily convert ideas into patentable innovations.

2.3. Technological change and more general market structures

The rigorous theoretical treatments in the literature growing from Arrow's work [7] have assumed that the invention process is monopolized. Thus the findings regarding relative incentives to invent are for differences in the invention-*using* industry only. The analysis of how competition *in* R & D affects performance is not addressed, nor is the impact of R & D on competition in post-innovation markets addressed.[3] Yet the Schumpeterian vision clearly encompasses such issues.

Recent theoretical understanding of the relation between technological change and more general market structures has grown from the insights of Scherer [264, 273] and Barzel [12]. Scherer

[3] For an examination of these restrictions in the context of the literature stimulated by Arrow, see Needham [205], who explores a firm's profit-maximizing demand-increasing R & D expenditures, given different conjectures about rivals' R & D and output behavior. Dasgupta and Stiglitz [50, 49] and Levin and Reiss [150] develop such conjectures in the context of cost-reducing R & D and close the model by imposing a zero-profit constraint. Their models are discussed subsequently.

perceived the crux of the positive economics while Barzel spelled out in stark form the normative problem. Fleshed out with the contributions of others, their insights provide both an analytical core and an agenda for ongoing theoretical research which in some cases refines their insights and in others seeks a new analytical consensus. In the following discussion, we first characterize jointly determined market structure and R & D behavior in a simple abstraction that clarifies the relation between the market outcome and the social optimum, and the links from structure and behavior to the outcome. The seminal works of Scherer and Barzel are then seen as special cases within the more general view that has evolved in response to their work.

Exposition of the theory of market structure and technological change is usefully begun by noting two *potential* problems with competition in R & D. The two problems, however, have opposite effects on the amount of R & D done, and hence may be offsetting.

The first potential R & D competition problem, **the overbidding problem**, arises in the pre-innovation market as competitors are stimulated to bid for the potential rewards. Suppose (1) that the post-innovation market will be monopolized, with blockaded entry; (2) that there will be perfect price discrimination (so the demand curve in Figure 1 is also the monopolist's marginal revenue curve); and (3) that the demand curves of existing products are unaffected.[4] These suppositions are made so that the gross private value, $\mathbf{V_p}$, of the innovation captured by the innovator will equal its gross social value, $\mathbf{V_s}$. Let that value, $V_p = V_s$, be $\mathbf{V}$, the present value of the stream of returns before deduction of any R & D costs. Although we shall quickly make the model more general, we first present the idea in the simplest possible framework from which it can be deduced.

One possible state of affairs is that for a single firm spending $\mathbf{x}$ on R & D, the value $\mathbf{V}$ can be obtained with certainty. With blockaded entry and no competition in the pre-innovation market, net social value, $V - x$, equals net private value, and no overbidding problem occurs. But suppose instead that we have competition with easy entry into the pre-innovation market—competition for the innovation prize. Further, suppose either (1) the value of the innovation is

[4] See, for example, Loury [162, pp. 405–406] and Barzel [12, p. 354].

expected to be shared equally by all successful competitors—their innovations will be substitutes, patentable or not; or (2) that there is only one winner in the race, and that the probability of a given firm winning, given that its expenditure is greater than or equal to **x**, is $1/n$, where **n** firms do competitive R & D. The firm's probability of success is zero if its expenditure is less than **x**. Then each of **n** competitors expects net profits of $V/n - x$, and with easy entry (ignoring lumpiness effects), zero-profit competitive equilibrium requires a value of **n** such that $V/n - x = 0$, or $n = V/x$. Net social value equals net private value, which equals zero ($V - nx = 0$). A variation of this problem was explained by Barzel [12], and we return shortly to his formulation of the problem.

The second problem with competition, **the appropriability problem**, arises in the post-innovation market. As competition in the post-innovation market increases, total *private* value, $\mathbf{V_p}$ (of the innovation with social value $\mathbf{V_s}$) is expected to fall. In a competitive equilibrium for the post-innovation market, revenues just cover post-innovation production costs. If that equilibrium emerged instantaneously, as would be the case in a frictionless world, returns to innovative investment (made in the pre-innovation market) would be negative. No firm would make innovative investments. The need for imperfection in the post-innovation market has been emphasized by von Weizsäcker [325] and is, of course, the conventional rationale for patents.

The first problem with competition, the overbidding problem, implies that in the absence of restraints, perfect appropriability would induce too much innovative activity in the pre-innovation market—even if sharing were probabilistic so that V/n is the "expected" return to one of **n** competitors. The appropriability problem, to the contrary, suggests that even a "perfect patent" may not suffice to promote R & D in a highly unconcentrated market. As the number of R & D competitors in the pre-innovation market increases, the more likely it is that there will be competition from substitutes, resulting from these competitors' R & D efforts, in the post-innovation market. Hence, because price competition in the post-innovation market intensifies, it is more likely that the value of the surplus of total revenues above post-innovation costs will fall short of the social value, $\mathbf{V_s}$. Firms doing R & D and competing in the pre-innovation market will expect something less than V_s/n in rents in the post-innovation market, since many R & D competitors means many competing substitutable products or processes in the post-innovation market, which in turn makes monopoly pricing—much less perfectly discriminating monopoly pricing—of the innovative output less likely.[5]

We can proceed from the foregoing observations to a simple abstraction that implies that monopoly can result in too much, too little, or just the right amount of R & D investment, and that more competition can move us either toward or away from the social optimum. In making these points with a simple abstraction, we shall also be able to explain the contributions of theorists whose detailed work implies the validity of our simple abstraction and the points we make with it.

Firms in the pre-innovation market would not in general expect a perfect price discriminating monopoly or cartel in the post-innovation market. Thus, appropriation of the entire social value from innovation will not in general be expected. Instead, the firms anticipate something strictly less than the entire area under the demand curve that would obtain in a competitive post-innovation market; and hence, even with no competition in the pre-innovation market, the pre-innovation monopolist would not generally invest the socially optimal amount in R & D, although that is possible. A profit-maximizing monopolist with full appropriability would behave as a social planner would, but full appropriability is unlikely. If we maintain the simple case where the given amount $\mathbf{x}$ expended on R & D wins *the* innovation, then as long as

$$x < V_p < V_s, \tag{1}$$

where subscripts $\mathbf{p}$ and $\mathbf{s}$ denote private and social values respectively, we get the socially optimal amount of innovation. But more generally, the present value of the expected stream of returns generated by an innovation is an increasing function of innovative investment. We develop this more general case using an abstraction following Dasgupta and Stiglitz [50]. The abstraction begins with

[5] Debrock [56] illustrates these ideas about market structure and optimal patent policy. In his model, more rivalry implies that optimal patent life is shorter, not longer as the appropriability problem alone would suggest. The optimal patent life is shorter because of the costs of duplicative R & D as firms enter the R & D race until expected profit from innovation is zero.

the present value, $\mathbf{V_s}$, of the expected stream of social returns (before deduction of any R & D costs) from an innovation treated as a function of the present value, $\mathbf{x}$, of the costs of R & D. We assume at this point either that the innovation does not cannibalize the surplus of existing products, or that a surplus remains after deduction of any cannibalized surplus. Given surplus from the innovation and a science base implying a non-zero probability of discovering an underlying invention, we expect the social value, $\mathbf{V_s}$, of expenditure on innovation to be greater than zero.

$$V_s(x) > 0. \tag{2}$$

Although we shall adduce ranges of the function for which it is not true that $\mathbf{V_s}$ increases with $\mathbf{x}$ at a decreasing rate, we can explain why $\mathbf{V_s}$ will change with $\mathbf{x}$ according to the relation shown in Figure 8; that is,

$$V_s'(x) > 0 \tag{3}$$

and

$$V_s''(x) < 0 \tag{4}$$

where ′ and ″ denote the first and second derivatives respectively.

There are three reasons to expect social value $\mathbf{V_s}$ to increase with R & D expenditures $\mathbf{x}$. Greater expenditures should increase the speed of innovation, the extent of innovation, and the degree of variety. However, we might expect expenditures to have decreasing effectiveness in these regards. The case of increased development speed is especially instructive. $\mathbf{V_s}$ might increase with $\mathbf{x}$ because greater R & D effort reduces the time until the innovation becomes available to users.[6] But although increased speed with which the innovation's returns begin implies $V_s'(x) > 0$, we expect $V_s''(x) < 0$, since it is reasonable to assume that still more expenditure becomes less effective in reducing development time. Indeed, there may be a minimum development time below which even infinite values of $\mathbf{x}$ cannot cause further speed-up.

$\mathbf{V_s}$ increases as the time to introduction, $\mathbf{t}$, becomes shorter since the discount factor

$$-d/dt(e^{-rt}) = re^{-rt} \tag{5}$$

[6] We note an exception below when we discuss Scherer's [256] model.

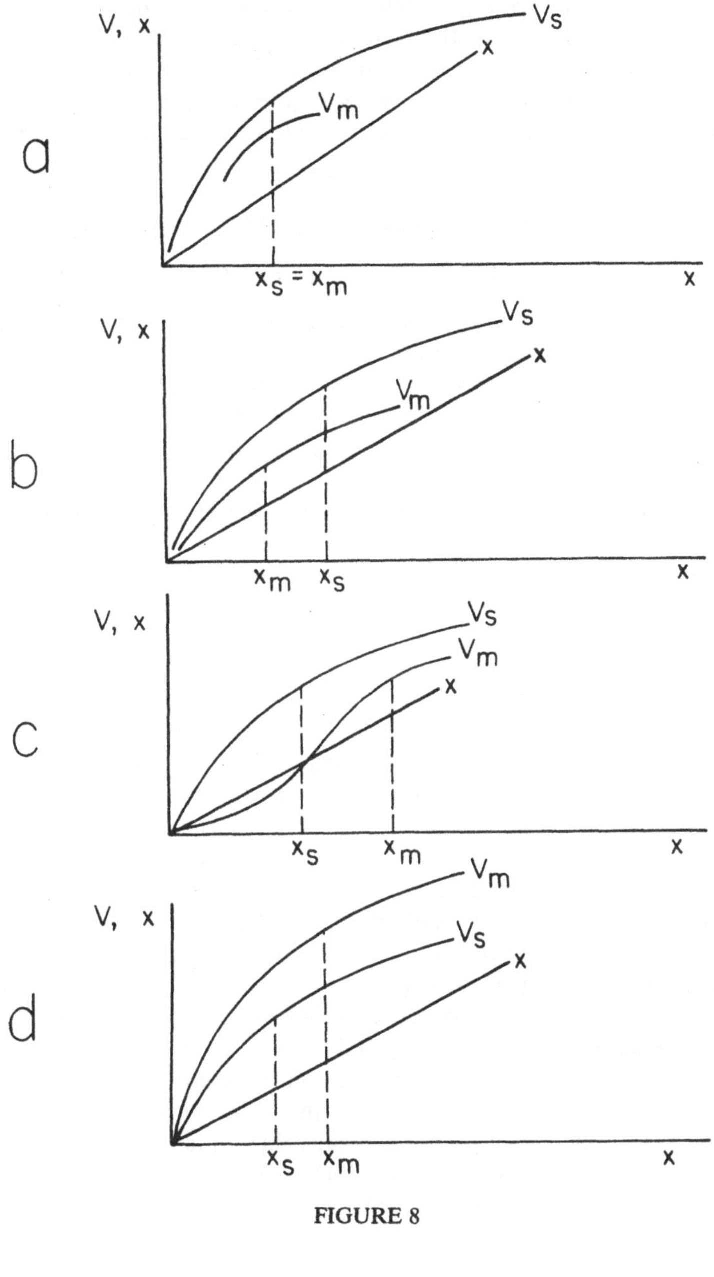
a
V, x
Vs
x
Vm
xs = xm
x
b
V, x
Vs
x
Vm
xm
xs
x
c
V, x
Vs
Vm
x
xs
xm
x
d
V, x
Vm
Vs
x
xs
xm
x

FIGURE 8

clearly increases as **t** gets smaller, where **r** is the discount rate applied. If regardless of the time of introduction, the benefit stream from innovation has constant discounted present value, **Z**, at the time of introduction, then the value of the innovation $\mathbf{V_s}$ is $Ze^{-rt^*(x)}$, where **t*** is the time of introduction given expenditure **x**. Then

$$V_s' = -rt^{*\prime}V_s \tag{6}$$

which is greater than zero since $t^{*\prime} = dt^*/dx < 0$. Further,

$$V_s'' = -rt^{*\prime}V_s' + (-r)t^{*\prime\prime}V_s. \tag{7}$$

The first term is clearly positive since $t^{*\prime} = dt^*/dx$ is assumed negative. The second term is negative if $t^{*\prime\prime} = d^2t^*/dx^2 > 0$ from the assumption that as time to introduction decreases, additional expenditures becomes less effective in further reducing that time. Scherer [264, pp. 360–361] provides the rationale for the relation between **t*** and **x**.

Thus, one basis for our general belief that $V_s'' < 0$ is grounded in the belief that

$$\frac{V_s'}{V_s} < \frac{t^{*\prime\prime}}{-t^{*\prime}}; \tag{8}$$

that is, as R & D cost increases, the rate of growth in value of the benefit stream is smaller than the rate of decline in the time-reduction impact of R & D expenditures. The time reduction gained from higher expenditures diminishes faster than the value of the time reduction grows. Since $V_s' = -rt^{*\prime}V_s$ by Eq. (6), the condition implies that $-rt^{*\prime}$ is less than $(t^{*\prime\prime})/(-t^{*\prime})$. Thus, *given* the technology of time-reduction (i.e., the characteristics of $t^*(x)$), the higher the interest rate, the less likely it will be that $V'' < 0$ because getting the benefit stream earlier has greater value at a high interest rate.

In Figure 8, the private value of $V(x)$ for a monopolist is shown as the curve $\mathbf{V_m}$, which, because of incomplete appropriability, lies below social value $\mathbf{V_s}$. Granting only the concavity of $V(x) - x$, any of the cases in Figure 8 is possible. Profit maximization occurs at the expenditure **x** for which the slope of the **V** function equals the slope of the **x** function, since then marginal value equals the marginal cost (one dollar) of another dollar of R & D. In 8-a, the monopolist invests the socially optimal amount, since the expenditures for which marginal value and marginal cost coincide are the same for both the social planner and the monopolist. Case 8-b is the one developed by Barzel [12] and by Dasgupta and Stiglitz [50]. In case 8-b, as in case 8-a, the monopolist cannot appropriate all of the surplus created by an innovation. Incomplete appropriability results because, for example, of the inability to capture all consumer surplus by practicing perfect price discrimination. Or the innovation may be accompanied by knowledge spillovers benefiting the innovative investments of other firms without compensation to the monopolist. The monopolist in case 8-b invests too little.[7] However, underinvestment is not caused by the divergence of private and social benefits *per se,* but by the *way* divergence occurs with $\mathbf{x}$. Both Barzel and Dasgupta–Stiglitz restrict their analyses so that underinvestment, as in case 8-b, is always the case. With both, the value to the monopolist is $V_m = \alpha V_s$ where the constant $\alpha < 1$. Hence, at any $\mathbf{x}$ the rate of change in $\mathbf{V_m}$ with respect to $\mathbf{x}$ ($\alpha V_s'$) is less than the derivative V_s' for $\mathbf{V_s}$. Given this *ad hoc* proportionality restriction, the monopolist always invests $\mathbf{x_m}$ which is less than the socially optimal amount $\mathbf{x_s}$. Of course, if cannibalization of the surplus of existing products (see Section 2.1) implies a constant $\alpha > 1$, the result is reversed, as in 8-d, in which the social and private benefit functions' positions are reversed. The monopolist spends too much on R & D. Further, there is no reason to preclude case 8-c, since the set of products available, complementary and substitutable to

[7] Lee [141] derives this result in the context of a search model. If the monopolist appropriates less than the full social value of innovation, the technology improvement just good enough to induce it to stop searching for even better technologies is less of an improvement than the social welfare maximizer's search-terminating discovery. Thus, the monopolist will undertake less search for new technologies. Note that in the special case of a straight-line demand curve and constant unit costs, society's payoff from having the innovation (including what would, given monopoly pricing, have been the deadweight loss, the consumers' surplus, and the producer's surplus) is always twice the non-discriminating monopolist's profits when they are not zero. If every outcome in the probability distribution of payoffs is strictly positive, then the social welfare maximizer looks at a probability distribution that is a translation to the right (over higher payoffs) of the distribution for the monopolist. In that case, Lee's result is a corollary of Theorem 17 in Kohn and Shavell [138, p. 113]. More generally, absent first degree price discrimination, the social-welfare maximizer's payoffs are in every state of nature greater than or equal to those of the monopolist protected from entry. Thus, Lee's result could be developed from theorems based on the utility of the probability distributions over payoffs [138, p. 114].

various degrees, will not be invariant with R & D spending and hence the time of introduction. Neither, then, will the relevant surpluses be; and thus, to assume $\boldsymbol{\alpha}$ invariant with $\mathbf{x}$ is unduly restrictive. The surpluses relevant to the monopolist are different from those relevant socially, and there is no reason to believe their relative magnitudes are unchanging over diverse levels of R & D effort and diverse innovation speeds.[8]

Thus, the fact that $\mathbf{V_m}$ is less than $\mathbf{V_s}$ for all $\mathbf{x}$ does not *per se* imply too little innovative investment by the monopolist. We know very little *a priori* about how the slope of $\mathbf{V_m}$ changes with $\mathbf{x}$, given the various reasons for incomplete appropriability; and therefore, we know very little about whether the monopolist in the pre-innovation market will carry out a socially optimal R & D plan.

2.4. Seminal insights about the positive and normative economics of market structure and technological change

Before we discuss later theories of oligopolistic behavior and R & D, we shall place the contributions of Scherer [264] and Barzel [12] in the perspective of the simple $V(x)$ abstraction developed above.

Scherer [264, 268] considered a market's representative firm facing competition in product R & D. Figure 9 derives the simple $V(x)$ function from Scherer's original n-firm parametric-rivalry framework. For the representative firm, $\mathbf{V_{p2}}$ and $\mathbf{V_{p1}}$ in the left-hand panel of Figure 9 represent alternative functions relating the private value of innovation to R & D expenditures, $\mathbf{x}$. $\mathbf{V_{p2}}$ shows the relation given greater competition than is the case with curve $\mathbf{V_{p1}}$.

Scherer's original abstraction treats the private value of the innovation as also a function of the time, $\mathbf{T}$, until the introduction of the innovation. The right-hand panel of Figure 9 also shows the present value of R & D expenditures, $\mathbf{x}$, as a function of $\mathbf{T}$. Figure 9

[8] One way to state this problem is that Dasgupta and Stiglitz, Barzel, and Lee assume the monopolist to face the same demand curve ignoring income effects as the social-welfare maximizer, but it chooses to produce less, given any technology, than the socially optimal amount. Our point is that in a general equilibrium context, the monopolist does *not* face the same demand curve as the social-welfare maximizer, and the relation between the two curves changes over time.

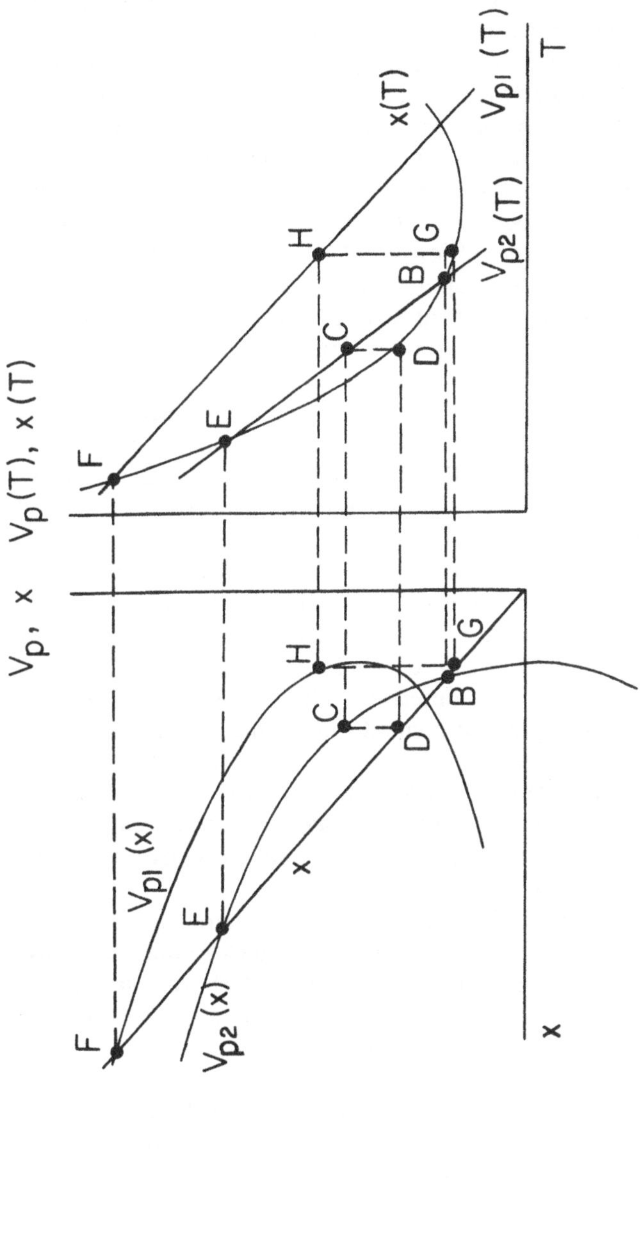

FIGURE 9

shows that Scherer's analysis includes cases where our convexity assumption does not hold. Finally, Figure 9 shows graphically how Scherer's original formulation translates into our own. In Scherer's conceptualization, with greater competition comes faster development and higher R & D spending because the private value function, $V_p(T)$, becomes steeper as the intensity of competition rises. An increase in the number of competitors in R & D increases disproportionately the number of post-innovation competitors anticipated in later periods. Therefore, competitive erosion of rents through time, preemption, and sharing of the total stream of benefits result in a steeper private value function for a firm facing more competitors. Thus, in Scherer's model, competition speeds the profit-maximizing development time (at which the marginal private benefit of a unit reduction in development time equals the marginal cost) for the representative firm, so long as reduced appropriability does not cause such a great downward shift in $V_p(T)$ that rents disappear altogether. For Scherer, then, the state of rivalry is parametric for any given rival. He could with this approach develop a rich feel for the positive economics of R & D rivalry. In his duopoly model, complete *inter alia* with the innovator's market penetration (new market case) or takeover (market-sharing rivalry) rates and the imitator's market entry or recovery rates and its penalty (a potential share erosion rate) for delaying imitation, Scherer considers asymmetries. He shows that as long as bottlenecks do not prevent a small innovating firm from exploiting the potential sales growth of an innovation, and as long as the advantage afforded large firms because of their established distribution channels and economies of scale is not too great, the firm with a minority market share finds it optimal to innovate sooner than a dominant firm would.

On the other hand, Scherer's minority-share duopolist tends to be a slow imitator. The larger firm is less quick to innovate, having less to gain by cutting into its rival's market share, but more quickly imitates, since it has more to lose than a laggard smaller firm. Baldwin and Childs [11] extend Scherer's model to consider cases where the profitability of being a "fast second" exceeds the profitability of innovating. In Section 4, we discuss further, in the context of diffusion, Scherer's innovator-imitator duopoly model and the extensions of Baldwin and Childs and others.

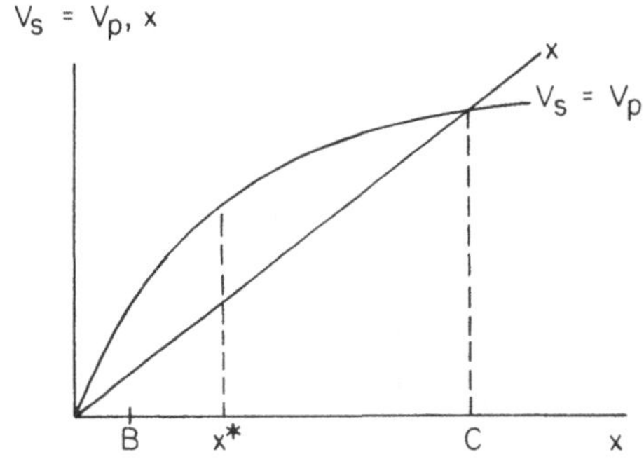

FIGURE 10

While Scherer's insights provided the breakthrough regarding the positive economics of market rivalry in R & D, Barzel's model [12] set out the normative issues. To put Barzel's model in the framework of Figure 8, we use Figure 10. As the innovation's introduction date comes sooner, we move from left to right in the diagram, since greater R & D expenditure **x** is assumed to accelerate development. Barzel's innovation can be had immediately and with certainty at a high enough "activating cost." The present discounted value of this "activating cost" is greater at earlier dates because it is paid out sooner (or additionally, in an expanded version of Barzel's model, because exogenous technological change decreases R & D costs over time). The present value of the sales minus production and distribution costs, $\mathbf{V_p}$, is greater the sooner the flow starts.[9] Bringing the introduction date forward to **t*** is

[9] In general, the concavity of $V - x$ depends upon the interest rate and the ease with which spending advances the introduction date. But that ease is not a factor in Barzel's model. In the growing demand scenario used by Barzel, $V - x$ is concave because bringing the introduction date closer gets diminishing rent for the marginal year gained because demand for the product is increasing through time. With Barzel, then, as we move the innovation closer in time, the present discounted value of the investment, **x**, rises. In Barzel's algebraic model, our **x** is Ie^{-rt}, where **I** is the constant cost of developing the innovation. Barzel (p. 353) observes that his model can be extended by having the investment required to introduce an innovation fall as the state of knowledge increases. Scherer [268, p. 431] keeps demand constant, but lets **I**, the cost of activating the process innovation, decrease through time because of advances in science. He thus preserves the concavity of $V - x$ via the supply side rather than the demand side.

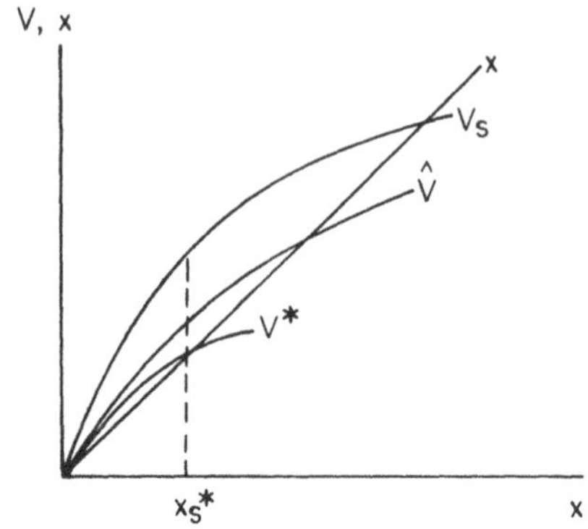

FIGURE 11

socially optimal and (because the $\mathbf{V_p}$ and $\mathbf{V_s}$ functions are tentatively assumed identical) privately optimal. However, competition in the form of free entry will bring the introduction date further forward (i.e., rightward) to $x = C$ in Figure 10, so that the private present discounted value, $\mathbf{V_p}$, equals the present discounted value of the R & D cost, **x**. With that amount of investment in the innovation, the internal rate of return on the innovation is equal to the opportunity cost of capital. The monopolist with blockaded entry and full appropriability will expend only **x***, since it is profitable to reduce the time to innovation only as long as getting the innovation sooner increases $\mathbf{V_p}$ more than it increases **x**. This corresponds to moving from, say, **B** to **x*** in the diagram.[10]

When the innovator captures all of the social returns as private returns, competition in Barzel's view tends to bring the innovation sooner (in general, tends to cause more investment in R & D) than is socially optimal. But there is an offsetting effect because of the inability of competitors (or monopolists) to appropriate all of the social value. Thus, Barzel explains, while free-entry competition

[10] The monopoly equilibrium condition in Barzel's model is then **t*** such that $hX_0e^{pt^*}e^{-rt^*} = hX_0e^{-(r-p)t^*} = S_0e^{-(r-p)t^*} = rIe^{-rt^*}$, where **h** is the per unit cost reduction because of the innovation, $\mathbf{X_0}$ is initial output, **p** is the rate of growth in demand, and other variables are as we have defined them earlier. He then divides through by e^{-rt^*} to get the equilibrium condition in flow terms: $S_0e^{pt^*} = rI$. Thus, rI is the carrying cost at interest rate **r** of an investment **I**, and flow benefits equal flow costs.

between would-be innovators tends to induce overinvestment, the innovator's failure to appropriate all benefits tends to result in underinvestment. In Figure 11, **V*** corresponds to a case for which the offsetting effects from imperfect appropriability and free-entry competition lead to the socially optimal amount of investment. The two forces just offset each other. In Barzel's model, this will occur if the ratio of social benefits to private benefits equals the ratio of the interest rate to the difference between the interest rate and the rate of demand growth for the product to which the process innovation is to be applied.[11] The key point is that a surplus of social benefits over private benefits is not sufficient to imply that the private market induces too little R & D. In Figure 11, the different private benefit curve $\hat{\mathbf{V}}$ (higher than **V*** because of greater but still incomplete appropriability) corresponds to a case in which the free-entry competitive equilibrium entails overinvestment in R & D despite incomplete appropriability.

Subsequent research has addressed issues opened up by the Scherer and Barzel contributions. Scherer explored various equilibrium solution concepts given duopoly, but his analysis left open for the general n-firm case the question of exactly how the equilibrium across firms would change as rivalry increased. As we shall see, Loury [162], Dasgupta and Stiglitz [50, 49], Lee and Wilde [143], Reinganum [240, 243, 248], Futia [75], von Weizsäcker [325] and Tandon [302, 303] have, among others, explored such equilibria.

Barzel, on the other hand, explored only two market structures—monopoly with blockaded entry and preemptive competition for the prize of being the sole innovator. His model also entails the purest form of certainty and no frictions in R & D. The blueprints are

[11] This result is a reworking in the context of Barzel's model of an idea exposited in Scherer's [268, p. 431] modification (see note 9 above) of Barzel's model. Using the notation introduced in note 10, for Barzel's model [10, equation (2), p. 350] the present value of the innovation net of capital costs is $\{S_0' e^{-(r-p)\mathbf{t}}\}/(r-p) - Ie^{-r\mathbf{t}}$, where S_0' denotes the appropriable royalty rate times the initial output. In the free-entry break-even equilibrium, that present value is zero; thus, $\mathbf{t}$ is such that $S_0' e^{-(r-p)\mathbf{t}} = (r-p)Ie^{-r\mathbf{t}}$. Now from note 10, in the social optimum, with the royalty rate equal to the unit cost reduction and a non-drastic innovation implying that price (and hence output) are the same before and after the innovation, $\mathbf{t}$ is such that $S_0 e^{-(r-p)\mathbf{t}} = rIe^{-r\mathbf{t}}$. If $S_0/S_0' = r/(r-p)$, then the value of $\mathbf{t}$ that solves the free-entry break-even condition is the same one that solves the social optimum condition.

available, as he says, and the innovation can be had immediately for an activation fee. As he notes, his model has no power in a world that is stationary—not stationary in the sense of no innovations, but in the sense that demand is not growing, or the activating cost is not falling. In such a stationary environment, either the innovation is profitable now, or it never will be. Once uncertainty is added, there is still an interesting optimality question even given unchanging demand (or unchanging innovation cost): how much to search. Socially optimal search requires that the marginal benefit of another trial (which is positive and diminishing) equals marginal cost.[12] As Loury [162] and Dasgupta and Stiglitz [50, 49] explain, competition in the form of free pre-innovation entry leads to oversearching—undertaking too many trials—unless the tendency to oversearch is outweighed by lower appropriability. Additionally, Barzel's certainty assumption ignores the impact on innovative performance of the interaction between competition and the extent to which firms' organizational structures are optimized for innovation. Klein [135] stresses that firms may take risks and create organizational structures to cope with risk only if forced to do so by the competitive pressures they face. To these and other works stimulated by the work of Scherer and Barzel we now turn.

2.5. The intensity of rivalry, uncertainty, and innovation

Kamien and Schwartz [123, 125, 124, 127, 129, 128, 130, 131] develop Scherer's notion of a representative firm, for which the degree of rivalry and other environmental conditions are characterized by parameters. They addressed both the positive economics issues raised by Scherer [264] and to some extent the normative issue emphasized by Barzel [12]. In their 1982 book [131], Kamien and Schwartz present a fairly general model that captures much of the essence of their earlier papers. We use it to explain their insights.

The representative firm of Kamien and Schwartz faces only market uncertainty—i.e. the uncertainty about when a rival will innovate. The firm can develop an innovation at time **T** for a present discounted cost of $x(T)$, where $x(T)>0$, $x'(T)<0$, and $x''(T)>0$. It is assumed that $x(0)$ exceeds $V(0)$, the present

[12] See Nelson [208, 213], and Evenson and Kislev [63].

discounted value of earnings conditional on immediate innovation. Although, by incurring more or less R & D cost, the firm can choose the introduction date for its new product, it faces a probability distribution over the time when a "composite rival" will innovate. Rivalry is greater, the greater the hazard rate $\mathbf{h}$, the probability density that "the" rival's innovation will be introduced at time $\mathbf{t}$ *given* that it has not innovated prior to that time. In the simplest model, this conditional probability density $\mathbf{h}$ is the same for all $\mathbf{t}$. An increase in rivalry is modeled as a proportionate increase in $\mathbf{h}$ constant over all $\mathbf{t}$.

To develop the model, let $\boldsymbol{\Omega}_1$ denote, at the moment of imitation by a rival, the present discounted value of the decision-making firm's future earnings from its own innovation. For the alternative case where the firm's date of introduction for its new product lags the rival's innovation date, let $\boldsymbol{\Omega}_2$ denote the present discounted value of the representative firm's earnings from the moment it imitates. $\boldsymbol{\Omega}_1$ is assumed greater than $\boldsymbol{\Omega}_2$, and both are assumed independent of the difference between innovation and imitation dates. Thus, although there is in general a penalty for introducing an imitation rather than an innovation (or, in other words, an advantage to being first), that penalty is independent of the innovation-imitation lag.

With this framework, Kamien and Schwartz show that two cases characterize the effect of stylized rivalry's intensity on the representative firm's chosen introduction time. In one case, greater rivalry (i.e. a higher hazard rate $\mathbf{h}$) at first increases and then decreases the speed with which the firm introduces its innovation. Thus, the representative firm's R & D expenditures as a function of rivalry take the form of an inverted "U". This case is similar to Scherer's model, since, as we can see in Figure 9, Scherer's model implies that, if R & D is worthwhile, more rivalry results in higher R & D expenditure up to the point at which the rents appropriated by the representative firm are no longer sufficient to cover the costs of innovation. As we show below, the model of Kamien and Schwartz yields the same result, given a particular parameter configuration. Thus for one case, Kamien and Schwartz predict an inverted "U" for R & D as a function of rivalry, whether continuous or with a discontinuous abandonment of R & D activity when rivalry becomes sufficiently intense. The analysis of Kamien and

Schwartz also suggests a second case for which more rivalry always decreases the speed of innovation, and hence R & D expenditure.

Recall that in Scherer's model there are two offsetting impacts of an increase in rivalry. On the one hand, the "carrot" of profits from innovation is lessened, because with greater rivalry each firm appropriates less of the total rent from innovation, sharing those rents with competitors. Further, greater competition in the post-innovation market can imply less rent to share. On the other hand, there is the "stick" for the laggard in new product introduction, since with greater rivalry, delay in one's introduction date results in a greater decrease in anticipated earnings over the next unit of time because of a higher probability of rival preemption. As long as the decrease in expected value is not so great as to eliminate profits altogether, at every time span to introduction, the erosion of rents causes the Scherer value function to become steeper (the absolute value of the slope becomes greater) as rivalry increases. As depicted in Figure 9, the slope of $V(x)$ is greater at any $\mathbf{x}$ in the relevant range. Thus, the time to introduction always decreases as rivalry increases up to the point where R & D ceases to be profitable. But in general, the slope of $V(x)$ need not be greater at each $\mathbf{x}$ as rivalry increases. Kamien and Schwartz and Loury [162] have adduced cases of a continuous inverted "U" and even cases where greater rivalry always reduces investment.

We develop the insights of Kamien and Schwartz using the following notation in addition to the definitions introduced above.

- ω_0 = periodic benefits from a product innovation in the absence of rival introduction.
- ω_1 = periodic returns from the innovation after the rival imitates.
- λ_0 = periodic returns from the old product prior to any innovation.
- λ_1 = return per unit of time on the old product during the period when the representative firm has not innovated, but the rival's new product has been introduced.

Although Kamien and Schwartz consider more general cases, we assume for concreteness that the probability distribution over the introduction date of the rival's product is exponential. Our representative firm then perceives the probability density function for rival innovation at time $\mathbf{t}$ as $f(t) = he^{-ht}$. Seen at time zero, the probability of the rival's product being introduced by time **T** is the cumulative probability[13]

$$F(T) = \int_0^T f(t)\,dt = 1 - e^{-ht}. \tag{9}$$

The probability of completion in the small period of time Δ—that is, in the next instant—is $[F'(t)]\Delta/[1 - F(t)] = h\Delta$. Then, **h** is the conditional probability density that a composite rival will introduce its innovation in the next small unit of time. For purposes of our numerical examples below, note that if we are to have a probability distribution over rivals' introduction time, **h** must be greater than zero, but it need not be less than one. For example, when **h** equals twelve, then the expected time of rival introduction is one month if time is measured in years.

If the firm chooses to introduce its new product at time **T**, it expects profits $V(T) - x(T)$, where, assuming that $\mathbf{\Omega_1}$ and $\mathbf{\Omega_2}$ are independent of the length of the lag between imitation and innovation,

$$\begin{aligned} V(T) = &\int_0^T e^{-rt}[\lambda_0(1 - F(t)) + \lambda_1 F(t)]\,dt \\ &+ \int_T^\infty e^{-rt}[\omega_0(1 - F(t)) + \Omega_1 F'(t)]\,dt \\ &+ \int_0^T e^{-rt}\Omega_2 F'(t)\,dt. \end{aligned} \tag{10}$$

As Kamien and Schwartz explain [131, p. 116], the first integral reflects the firm's earnings prior to introducing its new product, those earnings per unit of time being $\boldsymbol{\lambda_0}$ or $\boldsymbol{\lambda_1}$, depending on whether the rival has introduced its new product or not. The second integral reflects the firm's earnings after introducing its new product, conditional on that introduction preceding the rival's new product. Then the third integral must reflect the firm's earnings subsequent to its introduction time, given that the rival's innovation

[13] Note that the probability of the rival's success by time $T = \infty$ is $F(\infty) = 1$. The rival's expected time of introduction is $1/h$, since $\int_0^\infty t(he^{-ht})\,dt$, on integrating by parts, is found to equal $\{-te^{-ht} + (-1/h)e^{-ht}\}|_0^\infty$, which equals $1/h$, since $\lim_{t\to\infty} (-t/e^{ht})$ equals, by L'Hospital's Rule, $\lim_{t\to\infty} (-1/he^{ht}) = 0$.

preceded its own. In this instance, the firm is preempted at **t** prior to **T** and gets a stream worth $\mathbf{\Omega_2}$ at **t**, with probability density $F'(t)$.

Given the exponential form of $F(t)$ and, for simplicity, letting the R & D cost function $x(T)$ be $1/T$, maximization of $V(T)-x(T)$ with respect to the time of development **T** implies a value for **T** such that

$$(\lambda_0-\lambda_1)e^{-(h+r)T}+\lambda_1 e^{-rT}-[\omega_0+(\Omega_1-\Omega_2)h]e^{-(h+r)T}=-1/T^2. \tag{11}$$

In the special case of no previous products, we shall be able to explain clearly the essence of the link between rivalry and the speed of development. In that case, expected profit maximization implies that

$$[\omega_0+(\Omega_1-\Omega_2)h]e^{-(h+r)T}=1/T^2. \tag{12}$$

With $h=0$, i.e., with no probability of a rival innovating, the firm brings the innovation's introduction closer in time until the present discounted value of flow benefit, $\omega_0 e^{-rT}$ equals the marginal cost, $-x'(T)=1/T^2$, of reducing the time of introduction. How does the optimal time of introduction change as **h** and hence rivalry increases? After **h** changes and **T** is adjusted, the equilibrium condition must again obtain. Kamien and Schwartz find that if **T***, the profit-maximizing **T**, is less than a critical value $\mathbf{T^0}$, $\partial T/\partial h$ is negative and increased rivalry speeds development. Our simple version of the Kamien and Schwartz model can be used to illustrate conditions under which their conceptualization of the link between rivalry and the pace of innovation is essentially the same as Scherer's [264]. To show a condition under which, as in Scherer's analysis, more rivalry implies faster development up until all development ceases because expected profits are negative, we proceed as follows.

Considering the displacement from equilibrium, we find for our simple model for which there are no previous products,

$$\partial T/\partial h=\frac{e^{-(h+r)T}[\omega_0 T+T(\Omega_1-\Omega_2)h-(\Omega_1-\Omega_2)]}{2/T^3-(h+r)\omega_0 e^{-(h+r)T}-(h+r)(\Omega_1-\Omega_2)he^{-(h+r)T}}. \tag{13}$$

The denominator is positive by the second order condition for expected profit maximization. Thus, the sign of $\partial T/\partial h$ depends on the sign of the bracketed term in the numerator. If $T = T^0 = (\Omega_1 - \Omega_2)/[\omega_0 + (\Omega_1 - \Omega_2)h]$, then $\partial T/\partial h = 0$. If $T < T^0$, $\partial T/\partial h$ is negative; when $T > T^0$, $\partial T/\partial h$ is positive.

Now, first find **h** such that $\mathbf{T^0}$ is the optimal **T**. We do that by substituting $\mathbf{T^0}$ into the first order condition (12) and observing that **h** will be such that

$$e^{-(h+r)((\Omega_1-\Omega_2)/(\omega_0+h(\Omega_1-\Omega_2)))} = [\omega_0 + (\Omega_1 - \Omega_2)h]/(\Omega_1 - \Omega_2)^2. \quad (14)$$

Then the right-hand side of Eq. (14) is substituted for the exponential expression in $V(T^0) - x(T^0)$ to get expected profits when $\mathbf{T^*}$, the optimal development time, equals $\mathbf{T^0}$. These expected profits are zero when $\boldsymbol{\omega_0}$ equals $r(\Omega_1 - \Omega_2)$; they are negative (positive) if $\boldsymbol{\omega_0}$ is less (greater) than $r(\Omega_1 - \Omega_2)$. In the case where the expected profits at $\mathbf{T^0}$, given **h** such that $\mathbf{T^0}$ is optimal, are zero, less rivalry (lower values for **h**) implies a profitable $\mathbf{T^*}$ less than $\mathbf{T^0}$, and hence $\partial T/\partial h$ is negative. As rivalry, measured by **h**, increases, $\mathbf{T^*}$ approaches $\mathbf{T^0}$ from below, reaching it at the point where expected profits from innovation become zero. Thus, increased competition will always increase the speed of innovation if, for the quasi-rent flows, the difference between returns to innovation given the rival's imitation and returns to imitation equals returns in the absence of rival introduction.

Figure 12 provides the geometric representation, given that $\boldsymbol{\omega_0}$ equals $r(\Omega_1 - \Omega_2)$. It shows that the Kamien and Schwartz conceptualization and Scherer's model yield the same conclusion. Namely, so long as rivalry does not preclude positive expected profit, $T^* < T^0$ and more rivalry increases the speed of innovation. In Figure 12, imputing values for the parameters of $\omega_0 = 1$, $\Omega_1 - \Omega_2 = 10$, and $r = 0.1$, we see that $\mathbf{T^*}$ approaches $\mathbf{T^0}$ from below as we approach the tangency of $V(T)$ and $x(T)$.

In a Kamien and Schwartz model, a continuous inverted "U" relation between rivalry and R & D expenditures results if $\omega_0 > r(\Omega_1 - \Omega_2)$. In that case, as explained in the discussion immediately below Eq. (14), expected profit is positive when, given the degree of rivalry $\mathbf{h^0}$, expenditures $x(T^0)$ are optimal. Then for $h < h^0$, the optimal **T** is less than $\mathbf{T^0}$ and $\partial T/\partial h$ is negative; while for $h > h^0$, the optimal **T** is greater than $\mathbf{T^0}$ and $\partial T/\partial h$ is positive. Figure 13 illustrates this case.

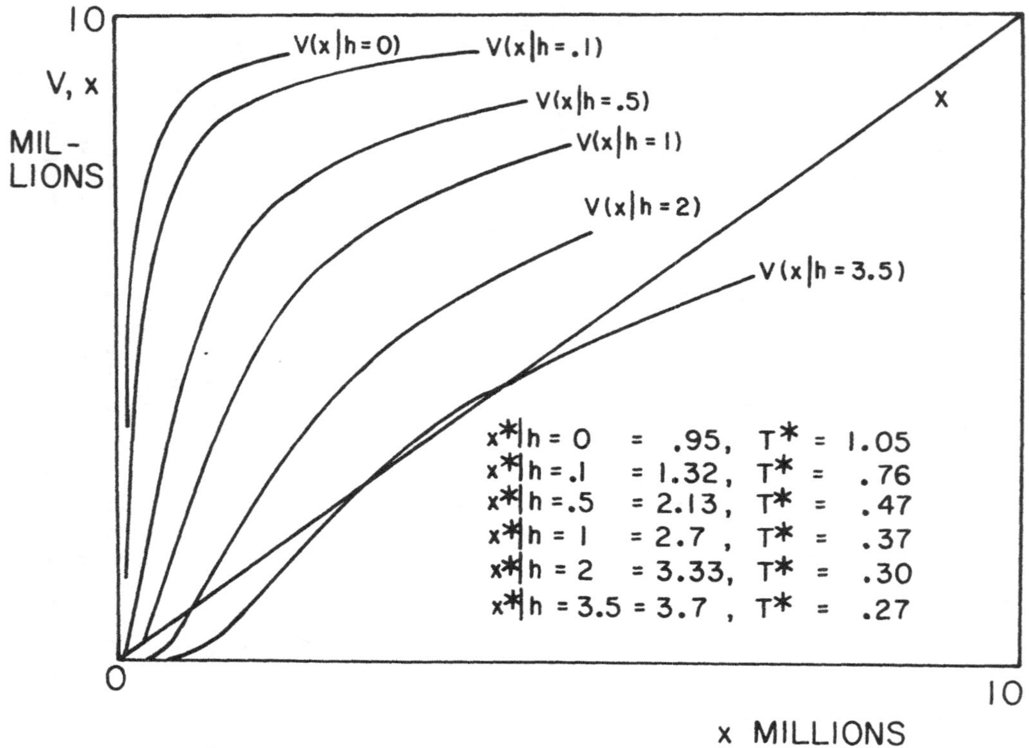

FIGURE 12 The case for which $\omega_0 = r(\Omega_1 - \Omega_2)$. **T*** is always less than $\mathbf{T^0}$ so that $\partial T/\partial h$ is always negative *until* the point where tangency occurs. Beyond that point further rivalry reduces R & D to zero. Here $\omega_0 = 1$, $\Omega_1 - \Omega_2 = 10$, and $r = 0.1$.

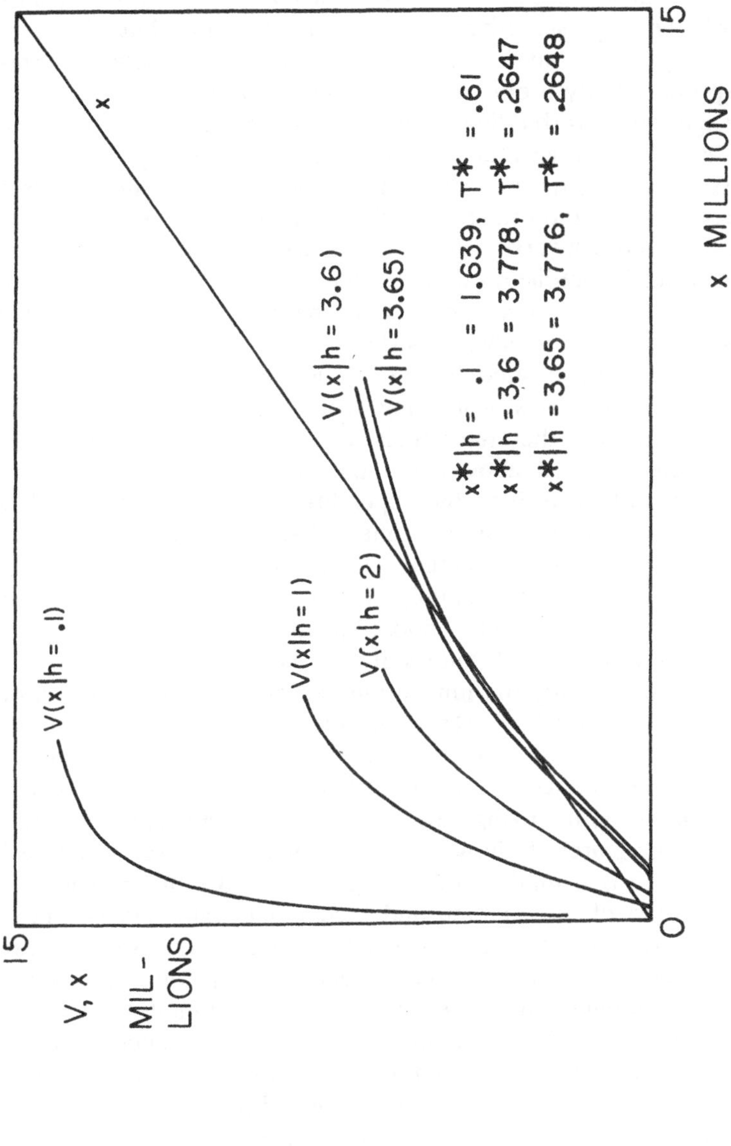

FIGURE 13 The case for which $\omega_0 > r(\Omega_1 - \Omega_2)$. $\omega_0 = 2$, $r = 0.1$, and $(\Omega_1 - \Omega_2) = 10$.

One can go on generating cases, and we do show others when discussing Loury [162] below. However, the key point here is that one can concoct models in which an increase in competition shifts inward the representative firm's $V_p(T)$ function but does not necessarily make that function steeper. In the most general terms, the appropriability problems created by increased competition may outweigh any overbidding problem, and more competition can decrease the representative firm's R & D spending. It is not necessary for the sharing, preemption, and appropriability effects of increased competition to steepen the $V_p(T)$ function as in Figure 9.

Kamien and Schwartz [131, pp. 123–124, 153–155] claim falsification of Barzel's prediction that the rate of return in equilibrium will be driven to zero. They insist that the firm's profit maximizing introduction time is always strictly later than the zero profit introduction time posited by Barzel, assuming free-entry rivalry. But their evaluation is misleading. They do not duplicate Barzel's assumptions, since they have their representative firm perceiving a hazard rate (defined above) and then embarking upon development, committing itself to the expenditures necessary to introduce its innovation at the optimal time. That is not Barzel's model. Barzel firms are not contractually obligated to undertake development. If preempted, they simply do not "activate" the innovation. Also, if Barzel's firm should choose any introduction time later than the break-even time, it knows it will be preempted by a rival innovator introducing the innovation earlier. A Barzel firm following the Kamien and Schwartz prescription would be preempted by a less myopic firm. The only equilibrium in Barzel's free-entry model is the one he adduces. Kamien and Schwartz firms are playing a game against an unmoving nature, while Barzel assumes rivals who will steal the march if allowed. In other words, market structure is exogenous in one model and endogenous in the other. An additional feature of the Kamien and Schwartz formulation is a more realistic development process, which for Barzel's firms was timeless.

In addition to addressing the impact of rivalry on the speed of innovation, Kamien and Schwartz have used their model to examine the impact of capital market constraints requiring financing through internal cash flows. They find that a self-financing constraint is limiting only when the innovation's expected profits are many times larger than current profits. They also relax the assumption accepted above that development is contractual in the sense that once the firm chooses the time of introduction **T**, it is locked into a contract with discounted cost $x(T)$. Under "noncontractual development," a firm may accelerate or decelerate its R & D efforts, even stopping them altogether, as a consequence of others' success. *Ceteris paribus,* project development is more likely to pass the positive profits test if development costs are not contractual, since the firm's costs can be cut when it is not first to innovate. Kamien and Schwartz explore many other complex variants to evaluate the relative profitability of imitation versus innovation. Their findings are discussed in our section on diffusion. They incorporate the effect of patents. They allow the innovating firm to modify the price of its new product, assuming the probability of rivals' imitative effort to be an increasing function of that price. And finally, Kamien and Schwartz [120, 125] explore technical uncertainty—i.e., when the firm is uncertain whether an expenditure of $x(T)$ will result in an innovation at time **T**. They obtain results qualitatively similar to what they find given market uncertainty only.

2.6. Responsiveness of rivals, conjectural interdependence, and innovative behavior

Kamien and Schwartz have analyzed the impact of generalized rivalry on a representative firm. But they leave unexplored important questions of active inter-firm rivalry, where one firm's behavior is influenced by the behavior of other firms, which in turn is reciprocally affected. Also unexplored in Kamien and Schwartz is the question of how the collection of rivalrous firms reaches some kind of market "equilibrium." There are two problems here. One is the nature of the rivalrous solution; the other is whether zero-profit equilibrium obtains. Scherer [264] considers rivalry, but does not impose the requirement of zero profits. Barzel [12] examines the zero-profit equilibrium, but has no real rivalry structure, since only one firm carries out the innovative investment. These questions are addressed in the work of Loury [162], Lee and Wilde [143], Dasgupta and Stiglitz [50, 49], and Reinganum [240, 243, 248], among others.

For Loury [162], market uncertainty comes from technological uncertainty. Each of **n** identical firms competes for a constant, perfectly anticipated perpetual flow of rewards $\mathbf{\Omega}_0$ which only one of the **n** will win. The winner is not the best performer in the customary sense, but rather the lucky winner of a roulette-type probabilistic process. Each firm makes a contractual commitment, with present value **x**, to R & D. But **x** does not imply certain introduction at time **T**; rather, the probability density at time **t** for introduction by the ith firm is $f(t) = \lambda(x_i)e^{-\lambda(x_i)t}$. Then, with $\boldsymbol{\lambda}$ denoting the conditional density of the firm's innovation being ready for market at time **t**, the probability that the firm's time of introduction is less than or equal to **t** is $1 - e^{-\lambda(x_i)t}$, and its expected time of introduction is then $1/\lambda(x)$.

Loury's technological relationship highlights the effect of R & D expenditures on the conditional probability density of introduction by the firm. It is conditional in the sense that it reflects the probability density of project completion, conditional on such completion by the firm having not yet occurred. Diminishing returns to R & D set in after the possibility of an initial range of increasing returns. That is, although $\lambda'(x) > 0$, $\lambda''(x) > 0$ if $x < \hat{x}$, but $\lambda''(x) < 0$ if $x > \hat{x}$. When $x = \hat{x}$, then $\lambda''(x) = 0$. When **x** is zero, $\boldsymbol{\lambda}$ is zero; when **x** is infinitely large, $\lambda'(x)$ is zero. Market uncertainty comes from this specification of technical uncertainty, since the probability that the representative firm wins the race depends on how much its $n - 1$ rivals spend.

Loury [162, p. 399] assumes no spillovers in R & D, so that the time of introduction by one rival is stochastically independent of the time of introduction by any other. Then the probability that the ith firm wins the race at time **t** is the probability that it succeeds *and* the others have not succeeded. That joint probability is the product of the probability that no rival has succeeded $e^{-a_i t}$, where $\mathbf{a_i}$ denotes $\sum_{j \neq i} \lambda(x_j)$, and the instantaneous probability that the firm succeeds at **t**, i.e., $\lambda(x_i)e^{-\lambda(x_i)t}$. Then the cumulative probability that the ith firm has been the first to innovate by time **t** is

$$\int_0^t e^{-(a_i)s}\lambda(x_i)e^{-\lambda(x_i)s}\,ds, \tag{15}$$

which, integrating by parts, is seen to be

$$\begin{aligned} Z(t) &= e^{-a_i t}(1 - e^{-\lambda(x_i)t}) + a_i \int_0^t (1 - e^{-\lambda(x_i)s})e^{-(a_i)s}\,ds \\ &= \frac{\lambda(x_i)}{a_i + \lambda(x_i)}(1 - e^{-[a_i + \lambda(x_i)]t}). \end{aligned} \tag{16}$$

Thus, Loury concludes [162, p. 399] that the firm chooses **x** to maximize

$$\int_0^\infty e^{-rt}\Omega_0 Z(t)\,dt - x = \frac{\Omega_0\lambda(x)}{r[a_i + r + \lambda(x)]} - x. \tag{17}$$

Recall that for the Kamien and Schwartz firm, the intensity of rivalry is a parameter **h**, a hazard rate equivalent to the conditional density of rival introduction. In Loury's model that parameter is $\mathbf{a_i}$, which if the probability of rival introduction is not zero, must be a number greater than zero (but not necessarily less than one). To illustrate how Loury extends the Kamien and Schwartz results, consider the simple case where $\lambda(x) = \ln(x+1)$. Then, $\lambda'(x) = 1/(x+1)$, $\lambda''(x) = -(x+1)^{-2} < 0$, and $\lambda(0) = 0$ and $\lambda'(x) \to 0$ as $x \to \infty$. Hence, in this simple case, $\hat{x} = 0$; i.e., diminishing returns prevail over all levels of R & D effort.

The firm's objective function becomes

$$\text{Max } V(x) - x = \frac{\Omega_0 \ln(x+1)}{r[a_i + r + \ln(x+1)]} - x. \tag{18}$$

The first order condition is

$$\frac{(a+r)/(x+1)}{[a+r+\ln(x+1)]^2} - r/\Omega_0 = 0. \tag{19}$$

Now, for a Kamien and Schwartz firm that takes the degree of rivalry, the conditional density of rival introduction **a**, as a parameter and chooses an optimal $x = x^*$, we can deduce that

$$\partial x^*/\partial a \gtreqless 0 \quad \text{as} \quad \ln(x^*+1) = \lambda(x^*) \gtreqless a + r.^{14} \tag{20}$$

Loury [pp. 400–401] deduces two cases. In one, greater rivalry always reduces individual rival investment; in the other, as rivalry increases, investment increases at first, but eventually decreases. The second case is illustrated in Figure 14, where (letting $\Omega_0 = 10$ and $r = 0.1$) we observe first an increase in **x*** and then a decline with increases in the rivalry parameter **a**.

[14] The displacement from equilibrium given by the first-order condition shows $\partial x^*/\partial a = (-1/A)[(x+1)(a+r+\ln(x+1))][\ln(x+1) - (a+r)]$, where **A** is negative by the second-order condition.

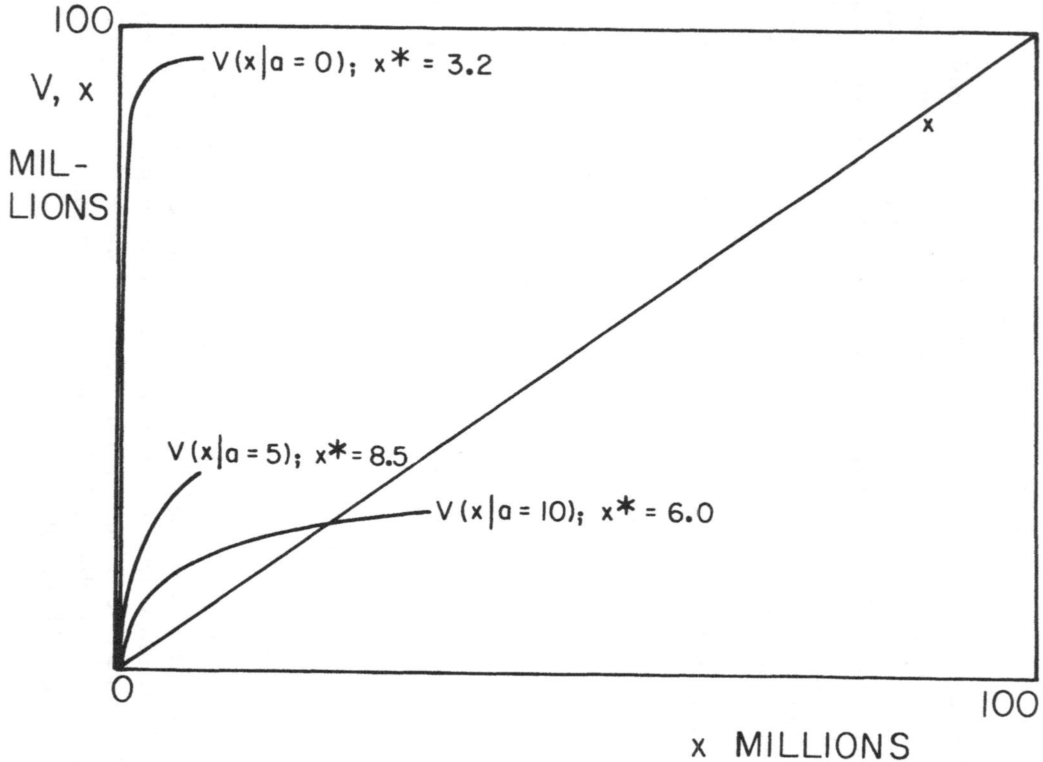

FIGURE 14 An Inverted-U for **x*** as a function of **a** in Loury's model with parametric rivalry of the Kamien and Schwartz type. $\Omega_0 = 10$ and $r = 0.1$.

But Loury then goes on to solve the problem left unaddressed in the Kamien and Schwartz parametric rivalry model. We cannot have depicted an equilibrium if, given the representative firm's choice of **x***, the other firms will change their R & D expenditures and thus change **a**. Loury accepts the Cournot assumption that each firm takes as given the behavior of the others. Then the symmetric Cournot–Nash equilibrium follows from the first-order condition

$$\frac{\lambda'(x^*)(a+r)}{[a+r+\lambda(x^*)]^2} - r/\Omega_0 = 0, \tag{21}$$

which determines **x*** as a function of **a**, **r**, and $\mathbf{\Omega_0}$. In equilibrium, each of the **n** firms must choose R & D investment **x**** equal to the **x*** which would be chosen, given that **a** equals

$$a^{**} = (n-1)\lambda(x^{**}).$$

Thus, to solve for **x**** as a function of any given **n**, given the parameters **r** and $\mathbf{\Omega_0}$, we substitute **a**** into the first order condition and solve:

$$\frac{\lambda'(x^{**})[(n-1)\lambda(x^{**})+r]}{[n\lambda(x^{**})+r]^2} - r/\Omega_0 = 0. \tag{22}$$

Figure 15 depicts this rivalrous solution. A value of R & D investment **x** denoted **x**** has been found such that each firm will find its level of R & D to be profit-maximizing in the Cournot sense.

Now, what happens to **x**** as the number of rivals **n** increases? In Loury's model with two or more rivals, **x**** falls as **n** increases. That is, $\partial x^{**}/\partial n < 0$, although total industry R & D investment nx^{**} will rise as long as Loury's "reasonable stability condition" (pp. 401–402) holds. Given our parameterization of the model, Table I shows that for $n \geq 2$, **x**** falls with **n**, but total R & D investment (and hence, the speed of innovation) increases. Table I uses the simple model with diminishing returns for all levels of investment. In this case expected profits would be driven to zero only with infinitely many firms.

Thus, in Loury's model, the individual firm's R & D expenditures vary in inverted "U" form as a function of rivalry, where rivalry is measured by the number of firms in the industry. In the typical case, beyond the peak of **x**** at $n = 2$, **x**** does not fall so fast with

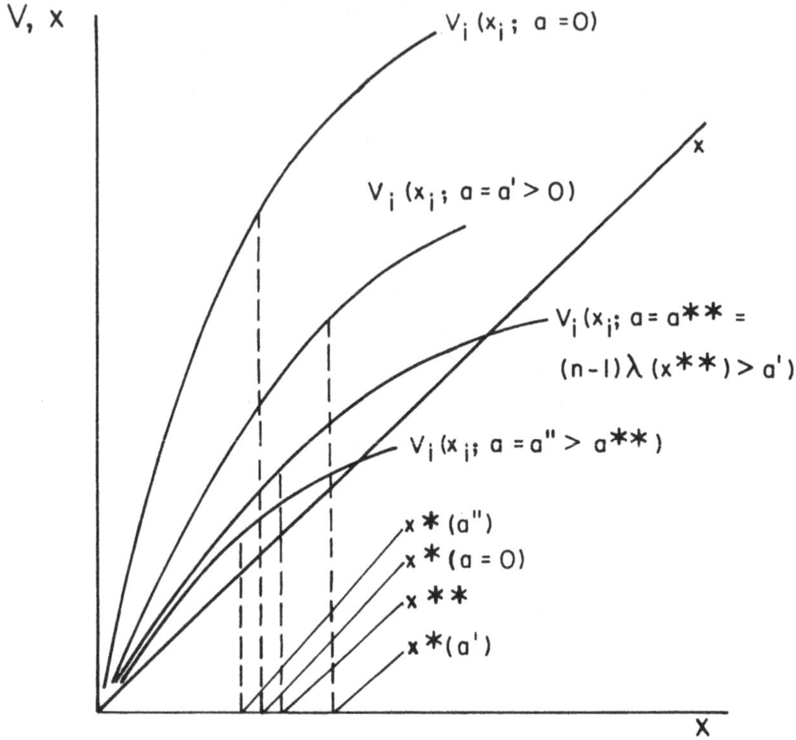

FIGURE 15 The rivalrous solution for R & D investment is $\mathbf{x}^{**}$ for the (ith) representative firm among $\mathbf{n}$ firms.

TABLE I
Loury's model: $\Omega_0 = 10$, $r = 0.1$, and $\mathbf{a}$, the degree of rivalry, endogenous

n	x^{**}	nx^{**}
1	3.2	3.2
2	9.6	19.2
3	8.9	26.7
4	7.6	30.4

n that nx^{**} also falls. Thus at the industry level, the story is similar to what we have seen before. Greater rivalry typically results in greater total R & D investment, and a faster expected time of introduction, as long as competition is not so intense that R & D is unprofitable.

The profitability of the equilibrium is a key point. If entry were free and fully divisible, profits would be driven to zero. In the special case where the technology for innovation has diminishing returns throughout ($\lambda'' < 0$), $\lambda(x)/x$ is greater than $\lambda'(x)$, and thus expected profits[15] must be greater than zero for any finite **n**. Only with an infinite number of firms will expected profits be driven to zero. In the more interesting case where the R & D technology has an initial range of increasing returns, the free-entry zero profit equilibrium will exhibit excess capacity in the sense that the firms will not exploit all the available R & D scale economies. Figure 16 shows Loury's diagrammatic presentation [162, p. 404] of this result. He conceptualizes the firm's R & D output as the conditional project completion density **λ**, which is a function of the R & D input of expenditure **x**. Expected total revenue is $V = \Omega_0\lambda/[r(a + r + \lambda)]$. Thus average revenue per unit of conditional probability density (that the firm's innovation will be ready for the market at time **t**) is $V/\lambda = (\Omega_0/r)/(a + r + \lambda)$, and marginal revenue is $(\Omega_0/r)(a + r)/(a + r + \lambda)^2$. For Loury, average cost then is x/λ, while marginal cost is $dx/d\lambda = 1/(d\lambda/dx)$ or $1/\lambda'$. His equilibrium at point **E** in Figure 16 is thus analogous to Chamberlin's monopolistic competition equilibrium [162, p. 404]. Average costs x/λ exceed marginal costs $1/\lambda'$ and there is "excess capacity" in the sense that the firm does not carry its R & D effort to the point where the unit cost of gaining time is minimized.

If we assume that the winner of the technology race appropriates the innovation's entire discounted social benefit, the model implies equilibria that are not socially optimal. Given any symmetric market structure with **n** firms, the industry equilibrium entails overinvestment in R & D. Following Loury [162, p. 406], each firm's ex ante profit expectation **π** equals $1/n$th of the social value. Assuming that social gains coincide with private profits, and given

[15] From Eqs. (17) and (21), expected profits are $[\lambda(x^{**})/\lambda'(x^{**})]\{[a^{**} + r + \lambda(x^{**})]/[a^{**} + r]\} - x^{**}$.

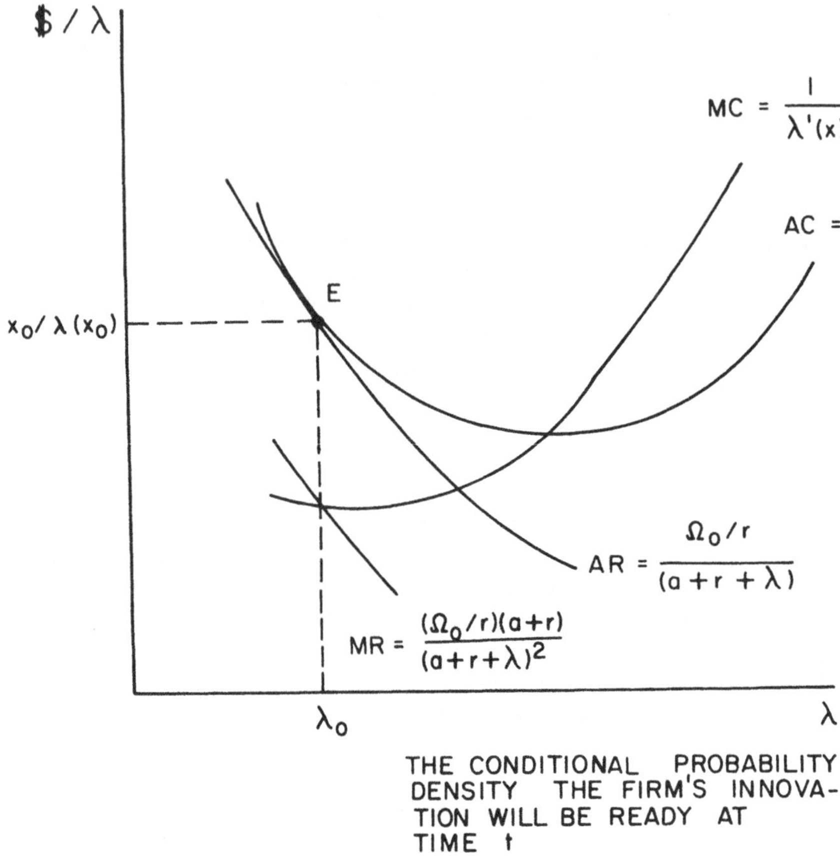

FIGURE 16 The excess-capacity zero-profit equilibrium in Loury's model. Each firm invests $\mathbf{x_0}$.

n, society would maximize $n\pi(a, x)$, where **a** equals $(n-1)\lambda(x)$. Denote the first and second partial derivatives of π with respect to **a** as π_a and π_{aa} respectively. And let the first and second derivatives of π with respect to **x** be π_x and π_{xx}. Then, social welfare is maximized when $(n-1)\lambda'(x)\pi_a + \pi_x = 0$. Since $\pi_a < 0$ and since in industry equilibrium $\pi_x = 0$, $(n-1)\lambda'(x)\pi_a + \pi_x < 0$. Therefore, since π_{xx} is assumed to be <0, $x^{**}(n)$ exceeds the socially optimal **x** given **n**. Thus, one welfare problem is a manifestation of what we have called the first potential problem with competition, a problem of too much competition in R & D in the pre-innovation market.[16] Assuming Cournot behavior, at the social optimum each firm will perceive that it can increase its expected profits by increasing its R & D investment, since π_x is greater than zero, and thus the optimum will be overshot.

A second source of inefficiency explained by Loury [162, p. 407] is that the socially optimal number of firms will in general differ from the number endogenously determined in competitive-entry, zero-profit equilibrium. Given the interesting case of initial economies of scale in R & D ($\hat{x} > 0$), unimpeded entry results in too many firms undertaking R & D. At the social optimum, each firm should undertake R & D expenditure such that average cost ($x/\lambda(x)$) equals marginal costs ($1/\lambda'(x)$), so that the average cost of gaining time is minimized. But in the Loury model equilibrium (1) each firm spends *less* than that socially optimal amount; (2) given the socially optimal number of firms, each firm would spend *more* than that socially optimal amount; and (3) each firm spends less as the number of firms increases. From (1), (2), and (3) together, in the equilibrium of Loury's model there are too many firms.

To remedy this problem, Loury [162, pp. 407–408] proposes an efficiency-inducing policy. The government would set a patent life such that if the number of firms were the socially optimal number, each would invest the socially optimal amount. It would then levy a lump sum entry tax or subsidy, equal to the expected profits or losses if the number of firms anticipating the authorized patent life were the optimal number. Then the long-run equilibrium would be socially optimal.

Several important modifications of Loury are suggested by, or have been made in, the works of others. Loury notes that his results

---

[16] Recall our simplest case for which an expenditure greater than or equal to $x < V$ would produce an innovation with total private value equal to total social value of $\mathbf{V}$ before deduction of innovation costs. With sharing of post-innovation rewards by $\mathbf{n}$ symmetric R & D-conducting firms, each firm expects $(1/n)V - x$. Net social value is maximized when only one firm invests, spending $\mathbf{x}$. But at the social optimum, each of the $(n-1)$ firms that spend nothing perceives that its expected profits (given expenditure $\mathbf{x}$ by it and the same expenditure by each other firm) will increase from zero to $(1/n)V - x$. In the industry equilibrium for fixed $\mathbf{n}$, each of the $\mathbf{n}$ firms spends $\mathbf{x}$ because each perceives that spending less or more reduces *its* expected profits. (More has no impact on expected gain before cost and less gets the firm nothing.) It is nonetheless true that society would gain if all but one firm spent less.

would be different if the model included imitation by rivals or the loss of pre-innovation market positions to the winner. As seen in Section 2.5, the models of Kamien and Schwartz provide a formal means of introducing the impact of R & D on pre-innovation markets; and Scherer's work on the breakfast cereals industry [267], discussed in Section 2.1, addresses the welfare implications of profit maximizing behavior by firms, given that some private gains are not social gains but merely cannibalize existing surplus. The insights of these several authors could be usefully included in a single model. Lee and Wilde [143] have modified Loury's model by changing the cost specification. Instead of a contractual commitment to a given amount of R & D, the firm's R & D expenditures include a fixed cost and a flow cost which stops once one firm innovates. Their modification allows more realism and some different detail about the impact of the number of competitors on the individual firm's equilibrium R & D investment, but, contrary to their claim, does not reverse Loury's excess capacity conclusion.[17]

Realism also requires relaxing the key assumption that there is only one winner of the R & D competition. The greater the number of pre-innovation competitors, the more likely it is that competing products will appear side by side in the post-innovation market. Multiple innovations will in general share in the post-innovation market. Stewart [296] relaxes the winner-take-all assumption in a Lee–Wilde model. There is then a post-innovation market share that, when anticipated as the winner's share by each of **n** symmetric, noncooperating competitors in the pre-innovation market, with losers sharing equally the rest, leads each of the firms to undertake innovative investment to precisely the extent undertaken by each firm in a cooperative n-firm cartel controlling both R & D and output. Hence, *assuming* that **n** noncooperating pre-innovation competitors *did* compete for a private payoff equal to the whole social payoff, it is possible for those firms to expect a post-innovation division of the market that induces them to invest the

[17] Lee and Wilde show that in their model, nonnegative profits require that $x/\lambda < 1/\lambda'$. They interpret this as the opposite of Loury's result, for which average costs of x/λ exceed marginal costs of $1/\lambda'$. But the interpretation is misleading, because in their model, average costs and marginal costs are not x/λ and $1/\lambda'$ respectively. In their model, average costs can exceed marginal costs and yet x/λ can be less than $1/\lambda'$.

social (and monopoly) optimum amount in R & D. Further, Stewart shows that the effect of rivalry, measured by the number of competitors, on the firm's equilibrium R & D investment depends in a well-defined way on the post-innovation market sharing expected. The results of Loury [162] and Lee and Wilde [143] regarding the impact of rivalry on equilibrium firm investment rates are seen as special cases with a winner's share of 100 percent. These models suggest that to understand the impact of the number of competitors on R & D effort, *even assuming that the total value of innovation (before R & D costs) is independent of market structure,* one needs to ask what determines the size of the winner's versus the loser's share.

Dasgupta and Stiglitz [50, 49] focus on the degree of rivalry in R & D (as well as rivalry in product markets) and the endogeneity of seller concentration. They emphasize that seller concentration is determined, along with R & D expenditures, by underlying market conditions such as the price elasticity of demand for a new product or the elasticity of unit cost of production with respect to R & D expenditures. Their models are highly abstract and use assumptions designed to facilitate the formulation of instructive analytical examples. For example, one of their prominent models [49, p. 276] (which has been developed and applied by Levin and Reiss [150]) assumes certainty of demand, costs, and the technology of cost reduction, and a purely symmetric zero profit equilibrium. The market is for a new product (how the new product was developed is not analyzed) and R & D is done to reduce unit costs. The assumption of a new product avoids the need to consider in a pre-innovation market competition of incumbents versus challengers. Regardless of the number of firms, Cournot behavior regarding both R & D and output is assumed. Then, for example, there is no allowance for the possibility that, for R & D or output, joint profit maximizing would occur with, say, two rivals while competitive behavior would occur with, say, ten rivals. Given the Dasgupta–Stiglitz assumptions, the number of firms and R & D expenditures must be endogenous and consistent with technology, demand, and zero profits. The industry R & D/sales ratio turns out to be proportional to the Herfindahl concentration index for a market with firms of equal size. The Herfindahl index is then $1/n$ where n is the number of symmetric firms. The constant of proportionality is the reciprocal of the price elasticity of demand. Simultaneously, industry R & D intensity is also a function of the elasticity of unit cost of production with respect to R & D expenditure. Thus, the endogenously determined number of firms depends on the price elasticity of demand and the elasticity of unit production cost with respect to R & D expenditure.

The Dasgupta–Stiglitz model then focuses on a rather "static simultaneity" of seller concentration and R & D expenditure. "Static simultaneity" implies the simultaneous determination of concentration and R & D, given a product and the technology of cost reduction. "Evolutionary simultaneity" would focus not on concentration and R & D behavior consistent at a point in time with zero profits and Cournot equilibrium. Rather, it would emphasize how the R & D evoked in a given market structure changes processes, products, and indeed the very process of doing R & D, and thereby shapes the evolution of market structure. The simultaneous equilibrium Dasgupta and Stiglitz describe is unlikely ever to obtain in an industry where R & D and technological change are important. Things change too fast for an equilibrium requiring one set of technologies and demands to obtain.

Tandon [303] develops the foregoing Dasgupta and Stiglitz model, assuming a new product which is not patentable, and for which the profits (sufficient to cover R & D costs) are divided among **n** symmetric[18] firms choosing cost-reducing R & D expenditures, given certainty of demand, costs, and the cost-reducing impact of R & D. Cournot behavior for both R & D and output and zero profits are assumed. This case is unlike the uncertainty case (e.g., Loury [162], Tandon [302], or Gallini and Kotowitz [78] among others), where "duplication" of expenditure in R & D with stochastic outcomes can have the desirable effect of raising the success probability, and where "wasteful duplication" entails going beyond the point at which additional duplication raises expected

[18] Although most models have addressed symmetric cases, Flaherty [70] has modeled stable asymmetric equilibria in an environment where cost-reducing investments are possible. The cost of acquiring extra efficiency increases with the current efficiency level, and the expense of cost reduction is assumed independent of the scale of production. Small-share firms have little output over which to realize the efficiency gains, and large low-cost firms face a high marginal cost for further efficiency gains. Thus, both the large low-cost firm and the small high-cost firm may choose not to pursue cost-reducing investments.

value by no more than it raises expected costs. Duplication in the Dasgupta–Stiglitz–Tandon certainty model is in itself purely wasteful socially. However, the duplication can improve economic welfare (as measured by economic surplus) because, with more firms in the industry, there is greater output and lower prices, with smaller static deadweight losses as n increases. The "competitive" (free-entry) equilibrium entails fewer firms as the elasticity of cost-reduction with respect to R & D expenditures increases, because concentration must be higher to allow the Cournot equilibrium to yield quasi-rents sufficient to cover the higher R & D costs privately optimal when technological opportunity is great. Principal conclusions of the model are that (1) the socially optimal number of firms is always less than the free-entry number; (2) that the cost reductions lost because of antitrust action reducing concentration will be greater in dynamic industries where technological opportunity is high; and (3) that in dynamic industries, barriers to entry are desirable (see also discussion of von Weizsäcker [325] below). Of course, working in the other direction is the possibility that secure firms may prefer to avoid risky R & D, and therefore that barriers to entry retard innovation. Klette and de Meza [136] observe that competition can increase risk-taking since a firm choosing a riskier strategy, that preserves its expected time of innovation while spreading out its distribution of innovation times, gains more from an earlier introduction than it loses from a symmetric delay. A greater than expected delay reduces the firm's probability of introduction at dates for which the odds are good that another firm will have introduced the discovery anyway.

Conclusions from the Dasgupta–Stiglitz–Tandon model conform with Schumpeterian views, but stringently special assumptions suggest cautious interpretation. The Cournot–Nash equilibrium in R & D and output, regardless of the number of firms, is restrictive, since conjectural interdependence can surely take other forms, and the form will vary with the number of firms. Their "one-step"[19]

[19] Brander and Spencer [28] compare such a Dasgupta–Stiglitz [49] one-step Nash equilibrium, in which R & D and output are simultaneously determined, with a case of "strategic R & D" involving a two-step equilibrium. Firms move further away from the joint-profit maximizing R & D choice, and, as compared to the Cournot equilibrium, there is more total R & D, greater output, lower prices, and lower profits. Although total costs are not minimized for the output chosen, net welfare may rise.

equilibrium precludes interesting behavior, such as sequential rather than simultaneous R & D and output decisions, that might well vary with market structure. The absence of patents is obviously restrictive. The research of the n symmetric firms is assumed to be purely duplicative, and thus provides a polar case relative to Klein [135]. Tandon [303] notes that modeling the impact of greater diversity of ideas is an important area for future research.

In the Dasgupta–Stiglitz–Tandon model, we see the tradeoff between the static allocative inefficiency of the Cournot equilibrium and an excess-capacity result analogous to Loury's. Firms crowd into the market and, at the free-entry equilibrium, prevent the attainment of scale economies in R & D. Given the assumptions, the social optimum corresponds to a natural monopoly with full appropriability and blocked entry, as explained when Barzel's model was introduced. Assuming full appropriability, the free-entry equilibrium entails too many firms.

On the dynamic question of how market structure evolves through time, Gilbert and Newbery [82] have opened up the question of whether monopoly will persist in a world of technological change that is induced by R & D. They note that if innovation is not drastic (i.e., does not result in a new monopoly for the successful challenger), the incumbent monopolist will preempt innovative entry by a challenger, because the innovation is worth more to the incumbent than to the challenger. This is so because if the monopolist wins, he receives M, the incremental monopoly rent from the innovation; while if the challenger wins, he innovates a substitute product or a new technology and receives a share S_c of the rents available, given two competing firms. Their pricing game is assumed to assure that total incremental profit shared will be less than the joint maximizing profits, M. M being greater than $S_c + S_i$, where S_i is the share going to the incumbent, $M - S_i$ is greater than S_c and the incumbent will preempt the challenger. If the innovation is drastic, there is no difference in incentives.

Gilbert and Newbery [83, 84], Reinganum [245, 246], and Salant [257] have explored the robustness of the preemption result. They consider alternative assumptions such as uncertainty, the timing of strategic moves, the absence of free entry, diseconomies in management, and transactions costs as the challenger bargains for exclusive rights to an incumbent's product and the incumbent bargains for the challenger's assets prior to patenting. Cave [33] develops a point of Salant's that the likelihood of inefficiences associated with preemptive behavior is lessened because of the opportunity for bargaining.

In the Gilbert–Newbery model, if the incumbent chose to spend less than the amount required for preemption, it would be certain to lose "immediately" its monopoly position. Reinganum [245] finds that when uncertainty is introduced, and the incumbent and the challenger simultaneously choose Nash equilibrium strategies in R & D, knowing that there will be a Nash output equilibrium should both survive, the incumbent will invest less, *ceteris paribus*. By delaying the expected date of introduction, the monopolist retains the old monopoly rent longer. This reason for delay does not, of course, exist for the challenger. In the nondrastic case, Reinganum finds an indeterminate bias in the incentives. The incumbent monopolist's incentive to delay innovation more and retain its old rents longer weighs against the Gilbert–Newbery incentive of a larger prize for being the winner. In the drastic case because the prize is the same size for either winner, there is only Reinganum's effect, making delay more attractive for the monopolist than for the challenger. For those reasons, while Gilbert and Newbery predict preemption in the nondrastic case and no difference in incentives in the drastic case, Reinganum's model finds that, on average, the challenger innovates in the drastic case, while there is no clear tendency toward preemption in the nondrastic case.

Harris and Vickers [101] develop the patent race between an incumbent and a challenger by emphasing their strategic interaction in the course of an asymmetrical race. Asymmetries have several sources. For example, the incumbent might value the patent more for the Gilbert–Newbery reason, or it might have more knowledge as Teubal [310] has suggested. Harris and Vickers emphasize the asymmetry caused by the incumbent's desire to keep its rival from winning. The incumbent may preempt its challenger even if it would not pursue the patent in the absence of the rivalry. Vickers [323] observes that the results about the persistence of monopoly do not carry over to analysis of the persistence of oligopoly.

Teubal [310] adds an important insight: preemption is more likely because, to experienced firms, later product generations can be more profitable as a result of the knowledge accumulated with earlier projects. Further, such efficiency differentials could constitute barriers to entry in the post-innovation market. Fudenberg *et al.* [73] address the preemption issue and find that all firms compete vigorously in R & D if they anticipate they are likely to be competitive, while one firm may preempt its rivals if it obtains a lead sufficiently great. In a two-stage model where firms first do research and then develop the results, Reinganum [247] finds that the leader in research and development invests less than the followers. In her model the rivals' strategies are inefficient from both private joint profit-maximizing and social welfare maximizing perspectives.

Reinganum [244] also finds a tendency toward more equal-sized firms, rather than toward monopolization, when she studies technology adoption in a duopoly with imperfect information. If product costs are sufficiently different, the high-cost firm adopts the new technology. Lee [142] uses the statistical theory of optimal stopping rules to explore a limited form of R & D rivalry pointing in the same direction. Given the set of known and potential technologies and the probabilities of finding cost-reducing technologies, the firm with the better technology will see further search as less likely to yield a payoff exceeding search costs because there are fewer superior technologies to be had.

2.7. Sequential innovation and evolution

Reinganum [248], Futia [75], von Weizsäcker [325], and Nelson and Winter [218] have all examined sequences of innovations and industry evolution. Reinganum [248] considers the behavior of an incumbent and numerous symmetric challengers, all maximizing expected profits over several periods. The innovations are sequential and drastic, with the losers at any given stage losing their R & D investment and receiving no reward at that stage. Reinganum finds that the incumbent invests less than the challengers, and hence has less likelihood of winning an innovation round, than if the winner were assigned purely by chance. Hence in this model of Schumpeterian competition, for essentially the same reasons as in Reinganum's version of the Gilbert–Newbery preemption story, one firm is unlikely to dominate the sequence of innovations. But as in the Gilbert–Newbery setting, Reinganum's results are equivocal if innovations are nondrastic. In detailed models of rivalry through time, Fudenberg *et al.* [73], consider the possibility that a follower disadvantaged at one stage can become the advantaged leader in a subsequent stage. The result emerges under the assumption that past R & D effort helps gain knowledge useful for future R & D. Nelson [213] and Teubal [310] discuss and use this assumption.

Futia [75] models Schumpeterian competition in a stochastic (Markov process) environment. Industry concentration and innovation are endogenous, determined by exogenous barriers to entry and innovative opportunity, the latter reflecting how R & D investment affects the probability of making the transition to a new product or process. Futia's "long-run equilibrium" is a "stochastic equilibrium" based on "the fraction of the time n firms are observed in the industry over any infinitely long sample path." [75, p. 682]. His model determines "the long-run expected value of the number of firms in the industry" (the inverse index of long-run concentration) and also "the long-run pace of innovation." Through his analysis, Futia explains the observed positive correlation between concentration and measures of innovative output or input. He shows that the long-run pace of innovation falls "on average" as entry conditions ease, but that easier entry conditions are correlated with the number of firms, and hence, concentration and the pace of innovation are positively correlated. Like many others, his model generates an inverted "U" relation between R & D intensity and seller concentration. There are two effects. Easier entry (negatively correlated with concentration) reduces the expected value of rents and lowers the pace of innovation. But for intermediate entry conditions, that effect may be outweighed by the "short-run" effect of an increased innovation pace as the number of firms increases. This latter effect is essentially what we saw in Loury's model as we went from monopoly to duopoly and the pace of innovation increased. But *here* more competitors reduce the total rents anticipated in the market, and that effect eventually reduces the pace of innovation as the number of firms increases. These predictions seem consistent with empirical regularities to be discussed in Section 3. And Futia's model also provides an explanation of the finding of Comanor [42] and Scherer [263] "that the positive correlation between the pace of innovation and concentration declines as the extent of innovative opportunity increases." [75, p. 693].

Futia makes several important assumptions. Size does not give a firm a cost advantage in doing R & D. The expectation of market power in the post-innovation market, not market power in a pre-innovation market, dominates innovators' incentives. Nash equilibrium obtains for the R & D game in each period, regardless of the number of firms. Entry barriers are exogenous (contrary to, for example, Levin [146, 147]). Only one firm wins each R & D race, and the winning product or process is "drastic" (a decisive improvement driving all competitors from the market, with subsequent entry via imitation restoring competition). There are no spillovers from R & D effort outside the industry.

Von Weizsäcker [325] begins his analysis of sequential innovation by observing that successful R & D creates opportunities for new innovations. He identifies the behavior of firms in "progressive" industries leading to a socially optimal stream of innovations. Such firms, he finds, must be protected to some specified extent from entry. The absence of sufficient protection causes too much post-innovation competition, driving revenues toward costs exclusive of R & D expense. With too much protection from post-innovation competition, on the other hand, there could be too much competition in the pre-innovation market and innovative firms might spend too much on R & D. For von Weizsäcker, an entry barrier exists if there is too much protection from entry to achieve the socially optimal allocation of resources.

Von Weizsäcker assumes that on average, the ratio of social to private benefits from innovation does not fall as the industry progresses through a sequence of innovations. Thus, the model does not treat mature "life cycle" cases in which later innovations add little to social welfare but shift sales to the innovator, implying a large (cannibalized) private benefit.

Von Weizsäcker's central conclusion, that faster growth for a progressive industry raises the need for additional protection of innovators from imitators, and hence stronger R & D incentives, is sensitive to his assumption that with increased growth, social benefits increase more than private benefits. Recall the Dasgupta, Stiglitz, and Barzel cases in which the monopolist appropriated only a fraction of the social value and hence spent too little on R & D. In the simplest models, the R & D shortfall increased as the discrepancy between social and private value increased. Von

Weizsäcker assumes that in rapidly growing markets, inventions are accelerated and the interval between successive innovations shortens. This shortening is in turn assumed to increase the ratio of social to private benefits, since with more sequential innovations over a given time interval, social benefits are increased, but more rapid creative destruction erodes the private return to a current innovation. If there is too little protection of innovators in a market, faster market growth will tend to make that protection even more insufficient. Thus, von Weizsäcker suggests that in rapidly growing progressive industries, barriers to entry (in the sense of his specialized definition) are unlikely (or at least, less likely) to be socially excessive.

These models of Schumpeterian competition are usefully contrasted with the vision of the 1982 book by Nelson and Winter [218]. Nelson and Winter explore a hurly-burly world in which profit maximization and market equilibrium are inappropriate or unattainable. Firms instead stake their fortunes on the use of rules-of-thumb. For this complex world, Nelson and Winter simulate the time paths of endogenously determined market structure and technological change. With their model, [218, p. 295]:

> [A] more competitively structured industry does lead to a poorer productivity performance than does an industry that is more concentrated. But the reason is not the one commonly associated with the Schumpeterian hypothesis: that best-practice technology evolves more slowly in the many-firm case than in the few-firm case. It is that there is a much larger gap between best practice and average practice in the case where industry capital is fragmented than there is in the case where it is concentrated.

The Nelson and Winter model does not yield the traditional explanations of how market structure and innovation are linked because it cannot—by definition. The model assumes that "the rate at which acts of imitation . . . occur is roughly independent of industry structure." [218, p. 295] To show exactly from where the key impact of structure on technological change comes in their model, we quote again at length [218, p. 295]:

> More specifically, the effect on average productivity arises in the following way. Innovative R & D effort yields, from time to time, superior techniques that temporarily define "best practice." The larger the innovator relative to the industry, the larger the immediate effect of such a technical change on industry average productivity. Similarly, when a new technique is imitated, the larger the imitator relative to the industry, the larger the impact on industry average productivity of each successive imitation of the new technique. In the model, the rate at which acts

of imitation (imitation draws) occur is roughly independent of industry structure. Thus the lessening of the effect of each individual draw, because of the smaller amount of capital affected when the number of firms is larger, is fully reflected in industry average productivity. For a given level of industry expenditure or innovative R & D, the productivity level associated with best-practice technique is independent of industry structure. But the gap between average and best-practice productivity is larger in the more fragmented structure because of the reduced scope of application of individual successes in innovation and imitation.

The Nelson and Winter story provides an original explanation of the correlation between seller concentration and productivity found by Scherer [271] and attributed by him to stronger incentives for R & D in concentrated markets because of greater appropriability. In addition, their results suggest one reason why observing that R & D/sales ratios constant with firm size do not necessarily imply that any firm size and hence market structure yields equally good performance—namely, because diffusion rates may differ. Of course, it is unrealistic to assume full diffusion within a large, monopolistic firm (see Salter [258], and the discussions above of Bain [8] and Fellner [65]). Further, as explained by Nelson [208, p. 363] and as emphasized by Klein [135], the monopolist may not be able to duplicate the efficient results generated by the ideal set of independent R & D endeavors.

Nelson and Winter provide intuition-sharpening examples of how market structure evolves through time as firms strive to survive in their uncertain R & D environment. They hypothesize [218, p. 311] that concentration will rise more rapidly: (1) the more rapid the pace at which technological opportunities expand over time; (2) (within limits) the greater the variance in successful R & D outcomes; (3) the greater the difficulty of imitating; and (4) the less the tendency of firms with large market shares to restrain their output growth as they grow larger.

Nelson and Winter also make an important policy point. They explain that even if we can pin down the relation between market structure and performance, structure is not an obviously manipulatable policy variable. Good policy needs to take explicit account of the fact "that structure is endogenous to a regime of Schumpeterian competition. . . ." [p. 333]. They teach that in an evolutionary setting, the costs associated with a concentrated progressive industry are several, including not only the conventional static deadweight loss, but in addition, the costs of the difference between average practice and best practice, and between best practice and the potential for technology not realized if R & D is inefficient [218, 219].

Nelson and Winter concede [218, p. 327] that "The model would be improved if it were generalized to reflect more of the systematic influences on industry structure—for example, technological economies of scale, product differentiation, and entry conditions. But there is no reason to think that the model, when thus modified, would somehow become unresponsive to the considerations we have explored in our experiments—or that the basic empirical strength of the stochastic approach would be forfeited." In [218, pp. 327–328], they argue that their results would remain robust if new entrants (excluded from their model) are more or less like the small firms already in existence. Their large firms would still be favored, and things would turn out much the same. However, everything falls apart "... if entrants came in at large scale, as technological leaders, and motivated by subtle, long-run strategic calculations." [218, p. 328]. They recognize that theirs is a "partial view of the matter." [218, p. 328]. In their models, oligopoly implies investment restraint, which has an impact on price-cost margins and the ability to get financing and thus ultimately on R & D policy. But firms do not base their R & D expenditures on conjectures about what rivals' R & D expenditures will be.

2.8. Discussion

Over the broad range of market structures, competition can lead to too much or too little R & D investment. The prospect of competition in the post-innovation market may erode expected returns and cause too little R & D investment, while competition in the pre-innovation market can cause firms to invest beyond the point where marginal social gain equals marginal social cost. The net result of these offsetting effects is not in general known, and it may be unknowable. A case can be constructed in which the socially optimal amount of R & D investment is undertaken by an expected-profit maximizing monopolist, given the special assumptions that the monopolist can pursue perfect price discrimination and that the social and private benefits of innovation, as well as the social and private costs, coincide. But under less restrictive and more plausible conditions, the monopolist or oligopolist providing a new product or process in competition with existing firms may appropriate less than the total social benefit from an innovation, or it may over-appropriate the benefits (by cannibalization). It may as a consequence invest too little or too much in R & D. The normative evaluation of R & D performance under various market structures appears to require a case by case approach.[20]

The literature offers a tempting generalization. More competition in R & D—i.e., more competition in the pre-innovation market—appears to increase the industrywide total of R & D investment up to the point where all such investment collapses because the expected benefit for the representative competitor (who knows that the chance of being a winner declines as more compete) falls below R & D cost. The generalization holds if the total private benefit is the same, regardless of the number of competitors in the post-innovation market. But the generalization is altered otherwise. If, as the number of R & D competitors increases, the number of anticipated post-innovation competitors increases, then firms can reasonably expect that price competition in the post-innovation market will erode the total private value of winning. In this case there is a more continuous inverted "U" relation between R & D investment and the number of competitors.

These insights have for the most part been developed in the context of models assuming that firms maximize profits, maintaining the Cournot conjecture that rivals will leave unchanged the levels of their decision variables. Many theoretical works accept that assumption regardless of the number of competitors. Further, firms are usually assumed to be symmetrically situated, and very little work has been done modeling first-mover advantages, although Scherer [264] pointed the way a couple of decades ago.

Models of Schumpeterian competition are only just beginning to make the degree of R & D competition an endogenous variable. Clearly, the analysis of R & D conduct and performance in various structural settings is only the beginning of the complete story, since innovative performance determines subsequent market structures.

[20] For an example, Debrock and Masson [57] conclude that in their model, the socially optimal degree of innovative rivalry cannot be determined in general, but rather depends on technical, behavioral, and structural parameters that vary from one industry to another.

Further, theorists are just beginning to explore the implications of knowledge spillovers among firms for the efficiency of market equilibrium (see Jaffe [114], Levin and Reiss [150], Reinganum [240], and Spence [294]).

Whether exploration of these issues will point the way to less contingent generalizations about the links between market structure and technological change is as yet unknown.

3. EMPIRICAL APPROACHES AND FINDINGS

3.1. Principal causal flows and variables

Economic researchers have hypothesized and tested many forms of interaction between market structure and innovation. But without doing too much violence to the range of contributions, the principal causal flows and variables investigated empirically since Schumpeter's seminal conjectures can be depicted in a simple schema such as that of Figure 17.

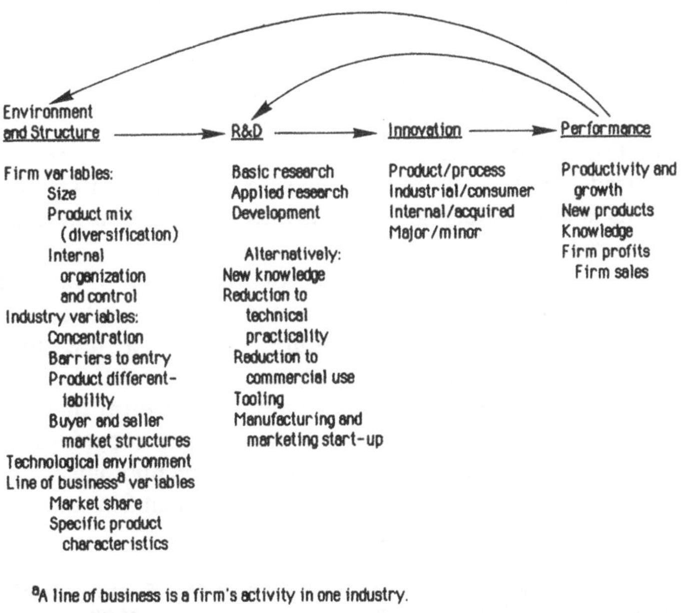

FIGURE 17 Schematic depiction of flows and variables in hypothesized structure-innovation relationships.

The effect of structure on innovation is widely recognized as indirect. The resources devoted to a firm's R & D effort are the input, while the resulting innovations, if any, are the output. Numerous studies have examined the effects of one or more aspects of structure on some measure of R & D input such as the number of scientific and professional persons employed, or the size of the R & D budget. In virtually all of these studies, the R & D inputs are implicitly assumed to be direct determinants of innovative outputs.

Almost without exception, later analysts have adopted a distinction similar to the one Schumpeter made between invention and innovation. Innovation was defined by Schumpeter as a change in a firm's production function, resulting either from production of a new product or introduction of a new production process or, in less rigorous terms, the economic implementation of knowledge and invention. Innovators are those who first make economic use of ideas or discoveries (inventions) they may or may not have originated. The innovator brings together and organizes a set of inputs to produce a new product and introduce it to the market, or to implement a new production process. In one of his earliest works, *The Theory of Economic Development* [281], Schumpeter envisaged an individual who borrowed all of the needed funds, purchased the rights to an invention made by another, set up a firm to exploit this invention, sold the firm as soon as it was established, and realized a profit from the proceeds of the sale after repaying the loan, thus acting solely as an innovator and not as a capitalist, inventor, or manager.

Figure 17 depicts two features of the relationship between structure and innovation that have not yet received appropriate attention in the empirical literature, despite a few insightful pioneering contributions. First, innovations feed back on structure, as well as affecting the subsequent amount and form of R & D, in large part through their impact on the economic performance of markets and firms. Second, the underlying technological environment influences the nature of interactions between firm and industry structural characteristics and innovation.

3.2. The formative period: interpretations of the Schumpeterian hypothesis and case studies through the mid 1960s

Much of the early work, following publication of Schumpeter's *Capitalism, Socialism, and Democracy*, relied on the most casual of empiricism [18, 76, 87, 151], as had Schumpeter himself. To cite one notable case, Galbraith [76, p. 93] asserted that "in the modern industry shared by a few large firms, size and the rewards accruing to market power combine to insure that the resources for research and technical development will be available." He went on to observe [p. 96], "The showpieces [of American industrial achievement] are, with rare exceptions, the industries which are dominated by a handful of large firms. The foreign visitor, brought to the United States by the Economic Cooperation Administration, visits the same firms as do attorneys of the Department of Justice in their search for monopoly." Given the paucity of published data on R & D activity available in the late 1940s and early 1950s, such appeals to anecdotal or impressionistic evidence are understandable. Nevertheless, researchers such as Maclaurin [169, 170], Stigler [297], Phillips [231], Stelzer [295], and Mueller [199] in the U.S., along with Carter and Williams [32], and Jewkes, Sawers, and Stillerman [116] in the U.K., demonstrated that through well-designed analysis of data published on other features of the economy, or intensive investigations of individual cases, it was possible to shed new light on industrial R & D and the sources of technological progress.

In a study of technological progress in 13 U.S. industries over the period from 1925 to 1950, Maclaurin [170] found high rates of progress associated with industries he characterized [p. 182] as having "high monopolistic qualities," or large size of price leaders and very difficult entry. But he concluded that "technological progressiveness cannot be correlated directly with the monopolistic features that I have singled out." Of greater importance were forces including the state of the underlying engineering art and the extent of entrepreneurial leadership by individuals with engineering or scientific training. He found support in this 13-industry study for a conclusion reached earlier in his work on the radio industry [169] "that some degree of monopoly is essential to technological progress," but "that some freedom of entry and the spirit of competition are stimulating to progress." [170, p. 182].

Stigler in 1956 found that labor requirements per unit of output, taken as an inverse measure of technological progress, had decreased from 1889 to 1937 most rapidly in those industries in which four-firm seller concentration had declined markedly, less rapidly in those in which concentration had remained low throughout the period, and least rapidly in those in which concentration had remained high. But in the same year, Phillips, using a smaller sample and observations from 1904 through 1939, found a positive and significant rank correlation between rate of growth of output per wage earner and the level of concentration at the establishment, rather than firm, level. Unlike Stigler, Phillips did not consider changes in concentration, but only the levels in both 1904 and 1939. Phillips cautioned that his results were equally consistent with causation running either from concentration to technical development or the reverse.

In a 1976 article drawing on a larger sample and using multivariate analysis, Greer and Rhoades [94] confirmed Phillips's finding and noted that when growth of output was added to Stigler's sample as a determinant of productivity advance, the relationship originally reported disappeared.

Stelzer, in a 1956 case study of the cotton textile industry, concluded that large firms with internally generated funds for research and smaller firms injecting competitive vigor into the industry were both required for desirable rates of technical advance. Mueller, in his 1957 analysis of the discovery and development of nylon by E. I. du Pont de Nemours, found both the research costs and the risk low, contrary to the Schumpeterian arguments respecting economies of scale in R & D and risk insurance through monopoly power.

On the basis of 152 usable case studies conducted among British industrial firms in the early and mid 1950s, Carter and Williams concluded that there were some advantages to size in the conduct of industrial R & D, especially in incentives to do basic research, but that an industry's scientific base—or the relevance of some scientific discipline to its operations and the resulting technological opportunities its firms faced—was the primary determinant of R & D activity. When the industries they studied were grouped into those relying on traditional, engineering, and modern technologies, the grouping accounted for most of the differences in conduct of R & D by firms and the extent to which they were successful in creating new products and processes. Other features of industrial structure were of little significance.

Unquestionably, the most influential of the early studies was that of Jewkes, Sawers, and Stillerman. Their conclusions were based primarily on a survey of 61 important inventions made in Great

Britain and the United States over the first half of the twentieth century. Their most widely cited finding [p. 82] was that "More than one-half of the cases can be ranked as individual invention in the sense that much of the pioneering work was carried through by men who were working on their own behalf without the backing of research institutions and usually with limited resources and assistance or, where the inventors were employed in institutions, these institutions were, as in the case of universities, of such a kind that the individuals were autonomous, free to follow their own ideas without hindrance." Twenty-one of the inventions they studied originated in industrial research laboratories, as compared to 33 attributable to individual inventors: the remainder could not be classified unambiguously. The inventions attributed to manufacturing firms were made in the laboratories of both large and small companies. Jewkes, Sawers, and Stillerman noted further [p. 88], "Even where inventions have arisen in the research laboratories of firms, the team responsible for it seems often to have been quite small. It is usually found that one outstanding figure has been surrounded by, and has stimulated, a few devoted colleagues in an intimate relation with his manner of thought and speculations."

Jewkes, Sawers, and Stillerman qualified their findings. Although invention could be carried out on a small scale, inside or outside of industrial laboratories, and although the laboratories of even the largest firms were typically small, *development* of an invention, or the stage of innovation, could be costly and require the resources of a large firm. But they questioned the overall significance of economies of scale and efficiencies even at the level of development. Rather, they suggested, inventions might be appropriated for development and commercial exploitation by large firms because of their superior financial resources and protected markets. Their conclusions were guarded, including a call for further study [p. 213]:

> To put it concretely, [it is suggested] that the ideal industrial organization for snapping up and transmuting inventions into serviceable products is that where the firm holds a master patent on an important invention, is confident that it can rope off for itself the fruits of development, and is dominant in the relevant field of manufacture.
>
> At this point, scepticism appears pardonable. For if, as suggested earlier, the large development costs of modern times arise partly out of the threat of competition, it seems inconsistent to assert at the same time that only under the security of monopoly will these large sums be spent.

The first publicly collected set of comprehensive survey data on

U.S. industrial science and engineering effort [316] was published by the National Science Foundation (NSF) in 1956. At first glance, the NSF data for the 1950s appeared to support the Schumpeterian hypothesis. In 1953, the first year surveyed, manufacturing companies with 5,000 or more employees had 40 percent of manufacturing employment but did 70 percent of the nation's industrial R & D work in the nation, measured by total expenditures. In the same year, firms employing fewer than 500 persons contributed 35 percent of manufacturing employment but only 10 percent of total R & D expenditures. The NSF's report for 1953 also found that companies with 5,000 or more workers employed approximately three-fifths of the scientists and engineers in manufacturing industries and were responsible for about two-thirds of company-financed R & D expenditures, whereas those same companies employed only about two-fifths of the workers engaged in manufacture.

However, when researchers focused on what was viewed as the Schumpeterian sector, or the universe of large firms only, support for the Schumpeterian hypothesis weakened. Schmookler [278] observed that the NSF figures for 1953 suggested that, among firms that conducted R & D, size had no effect on R & D spending as a percentage of sales. Worley [339] obtained directory data on the number of laboratory personnel employed by 198 "very large" firms. Classifying these firms into eight broadly defined industrial groups, he found six such groups in which company employment in R & D rose more than proportionately with the total number employed. But only two of the regression coefficients showed a significant departure from strict proportionality. "It does seem reasonable, therefore," he concluded [p. 186], "to assert that the evidence calls for a more convincing case for bigness than has so far been marshaled."

Subsequent statistical studies extended and confirmed Worley's scepticism. Using a much larger sample of firms with a far broader range of sizes (700 from a survey by the National Association of Manufacturers and 4,800 from a Harvard Business School survey), Horowitz [107] found that the fraction of firms with internal R & D facilities rose with both size and industry concentration, as did research spending as a percentage of sales. While the associations were statistically significant, the effects were small. Horowitz repeated Phillips's warning that the correlations he found were consistent with causation running from structure to R & D or the reverse. In an examination of 387 companies listed among *Fortune*'s 500 largest industrials for 1960 and for which information was available on R & D employment, Hamberg [99] found for the group as a whole a positive but weak association between R & D expenditures and size when employment was the size variable, but none when assets were used to measure size. When 340 of the firms were classified into 17 industry groups, Hamberg found only 3 such groups with statistically significant positive relationships between size and R & D intensity. Hamberg also correlated industry R & D aggregates with weighted-average concentration ratios and obtained a highly significant positive relationship.

More specific industry studies examining R & D output, or innovations introduced, were carried out along with the broader statistical studies. In a 1962 conference volume, Peck [229] reported that the pace of innovation in the aluminum industry accelerated after the structure changed from monopoly to oligopoly following a 1945 antitrust decision. In the same volume, Mueller [200] noted that only 10 of the 25 most important innovations introduced by du Pont between 1920 and 1950 were based on inventions made within the company. Of the 18 product innovations, du Pont made the initial invention in 5 and shared in one more. In contrast, the company was responsible for the inventions underlying 5 out of 7 process innovations. And Enos [62], examining major process innovations made in petroleum refining, found that in almost every case the original invention which led to the innovation had been made by someone familiar with the oil industry but not attached to one of the major firms.

Through a survey of trade associations and journals, Mansfield [174] ascertained the most important innovations introduced from 1918 through 1958 in the iron and steel, petroleum refining, and bituminous coal industries. He found that in petroleum refining and bituminous coal, the four largest firms accounted for larger proportions of these innovations than they did of output in their markets, while the reverse was true for iron and steel. His survey indicated three factors favoring larger firms: 1) a large investment required to innovate relative to potential users' sizes; 2) relatively large minimum size required for profitable use of the innovation; and 3) a large difference between the average size of the largest four and other potential users. In all three industries, Mansfield found that the relative contribution to innovation of the smaller firms was declining over time. Williamson [331] subsequently showed that the percentage of innovations made by the four largest firms in Mansfield's sample industries divided by their percentage share of the market decreased with concentration, at least beyond a critical four-firm concentration ratio of 30 percent. But the small and specialized sample precludes generalizing this observation.

In a 1965 study, Scherer [261] analyzed 448 corporations listed among *Fortune*'s 500 largest U.S. industrial firms for 1955. As an indicator of inventive output, Scherer used the number of U.S. patents issued to these firms in 1959 (allowing a four-year lag between the invention and issuance of the resulting patent). This number was regressed on measures of size, profitability, liquid assets, diversification, industry and technology classes, and seller concentration. Scherer's principal results included the following:

1) Patent statistics appeared to provide a reasonably satisfactory index of inventive output, despite differences in the quality of inventions as indicated by the value of the patent and in the propensities of firms in various industries to patent. Although the great majority of the patents were of low value, patenting was "fairly strongly" correlated with the number of R & D employees in a 352 firm subsample for which employment data were available. Further, similar firm-size relationships were obtained whether the number of patents or of R & D employees was analyzed. (In a 1969 article, Comanor and Scherer [43] further explored the validity of patent counts as indicia of innovative output by comparing patents applied for by and issued to drug companies with sales by the same companies of new drugs. Although the number of patents appeared to be a better index of R & D input than of output, the relevant correlations were all positive and significant. For further study of this question, see [179], [197], [259], and [280].

2) Interindustry differences, most notably "technological opportunity," accounted for about as much of the differences in patenting activity as did interfirm sales differences within industries.

3) Both cumulative rankings and regression analysis within technology and industry categories failed to support the hypothesis that

patenting increased more than proportionately with firm size. To the contrary, "If anything, the results show that firms below the half-billion dollar sales mark generate more inventions relative to their size than do giant firms" [p. 1114].

4) A diversification index, obtained by counting the number of industries in which each of the 448 companies operated, was used to test Nelson's hypothesis [207] that diversification should stimulate basic research and hence invention. The relationship between patenting and diversification was positive, as hypothesized, and strong. But there was reason to believe that the relationship was spurious, since the greater the degree of diversification, the more likely it was that the firm had some activity in a high opportunity industry. (McEachern and Romeo [193] subsequently provided support for this interpretation. They found that diversification out of petroleum refining, an industry with below-average R & D intensity, led to a significant increase in firms' R & D intensity; while diversification out of chemicals and drugs, both industries with above-average R & D intensity, resulted in a significant reduction in R & D intensity.)

5) Correlation of the intensity of either patenting or R & D employment with profits and liquid assets showed no significant relationship, thus failing to support the Schumpeterian contention that an attained monopoly position provides funds required for innovative activities.

6) Scherer also examined the effect of seller concentration on patenting by an industry's four leading firms for 152 such companies in 48 narrowly defined industries. The regression yielded a positive but insignificant relationship.

Thus, Scherer concluded [p. 1122], "These findings among other things raise doubts whether the big, monopolistic, conglomerate corporation is as efficient an engine of technological change as disciples of Schumpeter (including myself) have supposed it to be."

In a 1967 addendum [263], Scherer analyzed the relationship between R & D employment as a percentage of total employment and concentration for a 1960 *Census of Population* sample of employees classified into 56 industry groups. The relationship was positive and significant, even when dummy variables for technological opportunity classes were incorporated; but the correlation was much stronger in the traditional and mechanical technology industry classes than in chemicals and electrical equipment. Scherer attributed the difference between this result and that of his 1965 study to the more comprehensive sample and the inclusion of industries in the traditional technology class. Further, R & D effort appeared to increase only with lower levels of concentration. The relationship disappeared, and perhaps even reversed itself, when the four-firm concentration ratio exceeded 50 or 55 percent, hinting at corroboration of the inverted "U" relationship generated by several of the theoretical models discussed in Section 2.

Two surveys perceptively summarized the principal findings of research on market structure and innovation through the mid-1960s—an era during which scholars moved from early casual empiricism to systematic analysis of newer and more complete data sources and to more penetrating and sophisticated case studies. There was first a 1965 critical review by Markham [190]; and second, a book-length survey and summary assessment by Nelson, Peck, and Kalachek [214] in 1967.

Markham noted three fundamental conceptual points. First, and most central, he called for a clearer understanding of precisely what his teacher Schumpeter had hypothesized, and argued that the empirical findings of Worley, Hamberg, Mansfield, Scherer, and others supported rather than refuted a correct interpretation of this hypothesis. "The original Schumpeterian hypothesis," he observed [pp. 323–4], "simply stated that in the absence of uncommitted surpluses the undertaking of risky and uncertain innovational activities would not occur; and unless the prospective rewards to such activities were high (relative to competitive returns), the incentive to undertake them did not exist." This original Schumpeterian hypothesis "does not imply that the measurable innovational effort of a firm as expressed, say, in terms of its research and development expenditures should be a continuous and increasing function of market power, business size, or, for that matter, retained earnings." [p. 324]. Rather, he contended [p. 325], Schumpeter's theory must be viewed "as a 'threshold theory'; some departure from a state of perfect competition (or the presence of some monopoly) is a necessary concomitant of innovation, but it does not follow that twice this volume of departures, somehow measured, should lead to twice the volume of innovations." Others' empirical findings indicated that "The large corporation and some degree of market power appear to be concomitants of organized innovative effort, but corporate size and market power in excess of Schumpeter's threshold levels appear to be with us, and for this and other reasons are still legitimate concerns of public policy." [p. 332].

Second, Markham expressed reservations about the data and statistical formulations used by the empirical researchers, but went on to contend [p. 131] that the basic difficulty was "not so much their statistical as their conceptual inconclusiveness." In his view, the state of oligopoly theory, particularly as it dealt with non-price dimensions of business behavior, was such that "it is difficult to say much more about the statistical analysis of R and D than that it reveals far more stable and systematic relationships than those found for variables about which we are supposed to know much more."

Third, Markham thought it necessary to repeat the cautionary point stressed earlier by Phillips [231] and Horowitz [107], since the statistical work under review typically did not address the question of causality, even though the researchers presumed that they were testing the effects of size and market power on R & D rather than the reverse.

Nelson, Peck, and Kalachek described the underlying pattern revealed by analyses of the NSF data along with a possible source of misinterpretation. Across the economy as a whole, larger firms spent a higher percentage of sales on R & D than did smaller ones. But this was in large part because certain industries—aircraft, electronics, and chemicals in particular—were characterized by both higher than average R & D intensity and greater than average size of firm. Within individual industries, the relationship was much less pronounced, and thresholds were more apparent. "While in most (but not all) industries the R & D to sales ratios rise as one moves from the group of firms with less than 1,000 employees to the group in the 1,000–5,000 range, there is no clear tendency for these ratios to be larger for the giants in the above 5,000 range than for the firms in the 1,000–5,000 range." [p. 67]. Further, although at the time the NSF data did not include any separate size classes for firms with more than 5,000 employees, Scherer's 1965 article made it highly likely that there was no significant positive association between size and relative innovative activity beyond that level.

Nelson, Peck, and Kalachek observed [p. 67] that "in most industries there would appear to be a threshold on the size of an efficient program; if firms are not large enough to support a program of minimum efficient size, their efforts are *ad hoc* and informal or nonexistent." But empirical research had made it clear that there was no single threshold, either across the entire economy or for particular industries. "Rather," they pointed out [p. 71], "the optimum is a size distribution composed of small, medium, and large firms varying from industry to industry and from time to time." And further, they maintained, the optimal structure included "a rate of turnover among firms sufficient to accommodate enough new firms to prevent excessive traditionalism."

3.3. Since the mid-1960s: an introduction to empirical testing of reformulated versions of the Schumpeterian hypothesis

The observations of Markham and Nelson, Peck, and Kalachek bore witness to the types of questions most in need of investigation and to the problems of shedding much light on these questions by regression equations testing simple formulations of the Schumpeterian hypothesis. Further, the frontier questions did not seem amenable to deep exploration through the limited analyses permitted by the publicly available data. Prominent among such questions were the determinants of threshold size, the nature of dynamic business strategies toward R & D and innovation in various structural settings, and flows of causation in the complex interactions between market structure and innovation. The most promising empirical approaches appeared to be through case studies of specific firms or industries and the generation of new survey data in more detailed and usable forms.

The recognized need for reformulating the Schumpeterian hypotheses along with the growth of a quantitative tradition within economics have led to more sophisticated models and econometric techniques. These models, and the findings therefrom, can be grouped somewhat arbitrarily into three categories examining 1) the effects of firm and industry (and more recently, line of business) structural variables on R & D and innovation, 2) longer-run feedback effects of innovation on structure, and 3) the impact of the underlying technological environment on the relationships between structure and innovation.

The models formulated and the hypotheses tested in our first category are all "unidirectional" in one sense, and are often so in a second sense. The hypothesized relationships are all *causally* unidirectional, with a one-way causal flow running from one or more dimensions of structure to some aspects of innovative effort or performance. In addition, most but not all of these models are designed to verify and perhaps measure the strength of relationships in which the direction of the hypothesized effects does not change—e.g., R & D expenditure as a percentage of sales is assumed to increase with firm size throughout. (The model need not, of course, specify a linear relationship.) Threshold and inverted "U" models provide the principal examples of hypothesized relationships that are unidirectional in the causal but not the functional sense.

Feedback hypotheses follow the lead of Phillips and Horowitz, as well as the original Schumpeterian vision of creative destruction, in postulating a longer-term impact of innovation on industrial structure. Some analysts have sought to isolate and investigate this feedback effect, taking the shorter term effects of structure on innovation as given. But recognizing the feedback from R & D to the fortunes of firms and hence to market structures implies a need to frame more complete models, in which both structural and innovational variables are endogenous.

In a number of theoretical models, not only the strength but in some cases even the direction of the interrelationships between firm and industry structure and R & D are in turn dependent on other factors in the underlying technological environment. These models, as well as some work on diffusion reviewed in Section 4, have shown the need for empirical models with variables that capture the significant aspects of this technological environment, elaborating on the technological opportunity classes in Scherer's 1965 and 1967 empirical studies.

3.4. Firm size as a determinant of R & D and innovation

The structural hypothesis most frequently investigated is that relating size of firm to R & D. Other posited and tested structural determinants of innovation, apart from features of the technological environment, include market power, diversification, conditions of entry, internal organization of the firm, and, at a highly disaggregated level made possible by the U.S. Federal Trade Commission's

Line of Business Program, a firm's involvement in specific product lines.

There are in principle two sources of scale economies in industrial R & D. First, it may take a firm of a certain size to support and justify a particular R & D effort—to finance the program and make best use of the results. Second, there may be economies of scale in the R & D process itself, so that the innovative returns to R & D input increase with the magnitude of the effort.

In Schumpeter's own writings, as well as in early impressionistic comments on the general Schumpeterian hypothesis such as that of Galbraith [76], these economies were viewed as significant in magnitude and typical of modern industrial R & D. But Jewkes, Sawers, and Stillerman [116] were impressed by the modest scale of the R & D facilities of even the largest firms, while others asked whether large-scale R & D projects might be carried out on contract by independent organizations specializing in providing such technical services to industrial firms of various sizes [10, 107, 224].

Mansfield and his co-workers brought together reports of their studies in two 1968 books [178, 179] and one in 1971 [187]. In four out of the five industries they had studied, the largest firms spent less on R & D relative to sales than did somewhat smaller ones. In three of the four, the difference was statistically significant. In the remaining industry, steel, the largest firm's relative R & D spending was the greatest, but the difference was not significant. There was furthermore no evidence of general economies of scale in R & D performance. In Mansfield's words [178, p. 43], "where the size of firm is held constant, the number of significant inventions carried out by a firm seems to be highly correlated with the level of its research and development expenditures . . . . In most industries, the productivity of a research and development program of a given scale seems to be lower in the largest firms than in the somewhat smaller firms."

Mansfield's in-depth study of the R & D budgeting process in one large firm suggested a source of scale diseconomies. Those reviewing R & D proposals tended to discount both extremely high and extremely low profitability estimates made by the firm's research departments. This, coupled with a proclivity of the reviewing managers to favor proposals with early completion dates over longer-run but potentially more profitable ones, appeared to reflect a managerial coordination inefficiency in the larger firms rather than systematic adjustments to the discount rates applied. In their 1971 book, Mansfield *et al.* noted that in the chemicals, electronics, and machinery industries, large firms found it more costly to speed up projects than did small ones. As a possible reason for this cost difference, they suggested [187, pp. 223–4], "Insofar as time reduction requires a certain flexibility of approach a larger organization may be handicapped by inertia and by more difficult administrative problems. Even reaching agreement on how to proceed will take longer if more people and a longer chain of command are involved."

From such findings, Mansfield concluded [179, p. 217]:

> Contrary to the allegations of Galbraith, Schumpeter, and others, there is little evidence that industrial giants are needed in all or even most industries to insure rapid technological change and rapid utilization of new techniques. . . . Of course, this does not mean that industries composed only of small firms would necessarily be optimal for the promotion and diffusion of new techniques. On the contrary, there seem to be considerable advantages in a diversity of firm sizes, no single firm size being optimal in this respect. Moreover, the optimal average size is likely to be directly related to the costliness and scope of the inventions that arise. However, in general, these factors do not make giantism necessary. To repeat, there is little evidence that industrial giants are needed in all or even most industries to promote rapid technological change and rapid utilization of new techniques.

More recent work by Mansfield and his colleagues, reported in a 1977 book [185], reinforced the finding of no significant relationship, beyond a certain threshold, between size and either R & D effort or relative innovative output. Small firms appeared to play a disproportionately important role at the stage of initial invention and in early, relatively inexpensive R & D. In the industries studied, development, even though expensive, rarely required the resources of the largest firms. Further, the largest companies did not spend relatively more of their own funds on R & D than other firms of substantial size, although there were definite threshold effects.

A major methodological issue was raised in a 1973 article by Fisher and Temin [67], who interpreted Schumpeter's original hypothesis as positing increasing returns to scale in R & D with respect to the sizes of both the research establishment and the firm. They contended that empirical researchers had concentrated on a "Schumpeterian hypothesis" distinct from Schumpeter's own, namely that research inputs, or effort, should rise more than proportionately with size of firm. Tests of this so-called Schumpeterian hypothesis, they claimed, bore little resemblance to the original and neither corroborated nor refuted it. They approached the problem, as they saw it, by identifying two relevant elasticities. First, there was the elasticity of research input with respect to size of firm. According to Fisher and Temin, empirical studies claimed to have refuted the Schumpeterian hypothesis by showing that this elasticity was less than unity. However, support for Schumpeter's actual argument would have required showing that a second elasticity, that of R & D output with respect to firm size, was greater than one. Such an elasticity did not necessarily follow, they concluded, from either of the sources of R & D scale economies identified by Schumpeter (i.e., within the laboratory or the firm). As Scherer [273, p. 70] summarized their argument, "This [economies of scale in R & D] can have two effects. The cost-saving effect *per se* should lead to lower R & D outlays, all else equal. But with lower costs, firms may approve more projects, increasing outlays. Whether on balance the R & D/sales ratio rises depends on whether the elasticity of project approvals with respect to scale-related costs exceeds unity."

Scherer [265] criticized Fisher and Temin's article for failure to represent accurately the empirical work they attacked and for the neglect, implied in their use of added profit as the R & D output measure, of Schumpeter's vision of temporary monopoly eroded by imitation. Rodriguez [249] pointed out that in the Fisher–Temin model increasing returns to scale in R & D is inconsistent with profit-maximizing equilibrium in a firm of given size. But as Fisher and Temin noted in a reply conceding its correctness [68], Rodriguez's point heightens the difficulty of testing Schumpeter's original hypothesis.

Elucidating the core of the Fisher–Temin contribution, Kohn and Scott [137] specified a production function for R & D output to replace Fisher and Temin's incremental profit measure of this output. Kohn and Scott demonstrated that it is possible to have increasing returns to R & D input and hence decreasing marginal R & D cost at equilibrium, provided the marginal value added by R & D is falling more rapidly than its marginal cost. They offered two definitions of the extent to which an industry may be considered "Schumpeterian." The greater the elasticity of (declining) marginal

R & D cost with respect to the output of R & D, the more "Schumpeterian" the industry is in the cost sense. And the greater the marginal value added by R & D with respect to the size of the firm, the more "Schumpeterian" the industry is in the productivity sense. Under this interpretation of Schumpeter's original hypothesis—one that seems more faithful to Schumpeter's vision—Kohn and Scott discovered conditions such that an elasticity of R & D input with respect to firm size of greater than one (the putative "Schumpeterian hypothesis") does imply an elasticity of R & D output with respect to size of greater than one ("Schumpeter's own hypothesis").

The Kohn–Scott analysis leads to an important methodological caveat. Empirical estimates of how "Schumpeterian" an industry is can be made by measuring the elasticity of R & D with respect to firm size at equilibrium, provided the firms face similar R & D cost and productivity conditions. But in the absence of uniform conditions, data on individual firms cannot be used to test a cross-sectional relationship between size and any measure of R & D activity. In Figure 18, illustrating this point, f_1 and f_2 are dissimilar functions relating value of R & D output (V_r) to size of firm (S) for each of two firms. Both exhibit increasing returns to R & D scale in the Fisher–Temin sense—and hence as Schumpeter hypothesized. E_1 and E_2 are profit-maximizing equilibria for the two firms. The relevant elasticities $\epsilon = (dV_r/dS) \cdot (S/V_r)$ are identical at E_1 and E_2, since by construction the smaller slope at E_2 is just offset by the larger ratio of firm size to value of R & D output. Fitting a line such as the dashed line in Figure 11 through cross-sectionally observed points such as E_1 and E_2 could yield the appearance of an elasticity of less than one, or possibly even an inverse relationship and negative elasticity, belying the actual individual firm elasticities at E_1 and E_2.

In a 1965 article, Comanor [41] attacked the question of R & D scale economies in the pharmaceutical industry, measuring innovative output as sales revenue derived from new chemical entities (representing major innovations) and all new products for the first two calendar years after introduction. The scale of R & D input, or effort, was measured by the number of professional personnel or total research personnel employed by a company. Firm size was measured as total sales. Comanor found that there were substantial

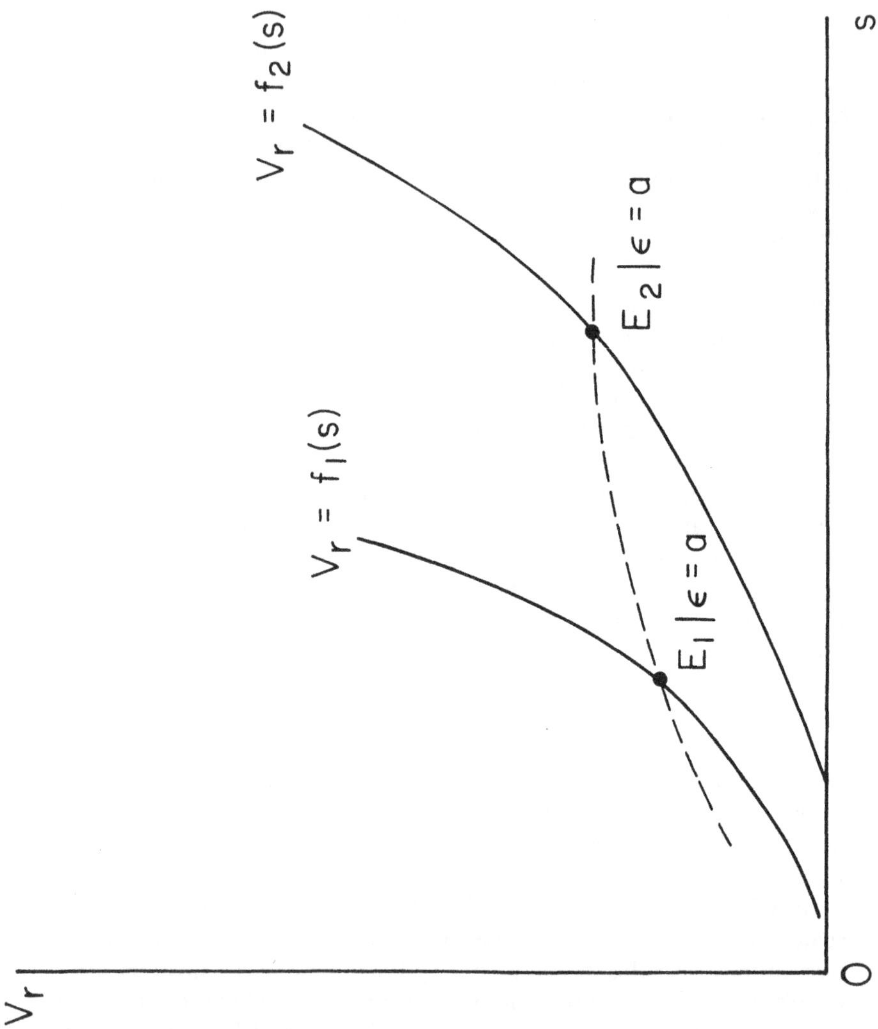

FIGURE 18 Actual and spuriously observed elasticities of value added by R & D

economies of scale among the smaller of the 157 firms in his sample, but diseconomies among the larger ones. His measured elasticity of new entity sales with respect to R & D effort was 1.39 at annual total sales of $1 million, 0.61 at $10 million, and 0.54 at $50 million.

Comanor's results for the pharmaceutical industry were extended in a 1968 study by Grabowski [90], which also examined the chemicals and petroleum refining industries. His regressions of R & D intensity on firm size yielded contrasting results for the two most research-intensive of his industries, chemicals and drugs, with a significantly positive relationship for chemicals and a negative one for drugs. A plotted graph showed, however, that in the case of drugs R & D intensity first rose and then fell with size in an inverted "U."

No other industry has been examined with respect to structure and innovation as often as pharmaceuticals. There was a flurry of articles in the mid-1970s, stimulated largely by passage of 1962 amendments to the U.S. Food, Drug, and Cosmetic Act, which greatly increased federal regulation of new drug testing and marketing. Greater regulation, it was shown, made R & D both more costly and more risky. Vernon and Gusen [320], Grabowski and Vernon [93], and Schwartzman [286] all found that pharmaceutical R & D became more concentrated, and that a positive relationship between size and relative R & D effort emerged after 1962. But Loeb and Lin [160], using post-1962 data and an exponential equation, obtained a result similar to the one plotted in Grabowski's 1968 paper: R & D intensity increased with size up to a point, followed by an inverse relationship at very large sizes.

Studies of other industries yielded suggestive and significant insights. In an update of Peck's 1962 aluminum industry study, Smith [290] found that in 1971 the large primary producers carried out the bulk of the activity in only one innovation class, alloys; while their suppliers and customers—equipment manufacturers, independent fabricators, and end-product manufacturers, many of them small firms—accounted for virtually all of the new product development in fabricating, joining, and finishing. Imel, Behr, and Helmberger [110] found that company-funded R & D/sales ratios did not rise significantly with firm size in the food processing industries. But in estimating a quadratic function for the food industries, Culbertson and Mueller [48] found a distinct threshold effect of firm size on the rate of increase of R & D employment, R & D expenditures, and patents assigned to the firm, in a sample ranging in size from $20 million to $1,012 million in assets. The inflection point, or threshold, was reached at $126 to $149 million in assets. Brock [30] noted that IBM originated or played a leading role in only 7 of 23 major innovations in the computer industry while dominating the market. Technical progress in that industry, he added, relied heavily on outside advances, particularly in semiconductor technology. Webbink [327] found what he characterized as limited evidence that in the research-intensive semiconductor industry both R & D expenditures and patents rose less than proportionately with company sales. In an examination of 101 firms from the chemicals industry, Link [152] found the rate of return on R & D expenditures rose with firm size. However, beyond a threshold size of approximately $300 million annual sales, there were no further increases in rate of return with size.

Studies of market structure and innovation using data from other industrialized countries largely confirmed the findings emerging from work with U.S. data, notably the lack of evidence of a clearcut causal relationship beyond a size threshold running from firm size to innovative activity.

Uhlman's study [313], carried out in West Germany's Ifo-Institut für Wirtschaftsforschung, found that among surveyed enterprises with less than 1,000 employees or annual sales of less than DM150 million in that nation's manufacturing industries, only about one fourth were engaged in R & D in 1975, while virtually all of those with over 1,000 employees did have R & D programs. Another Ifo-Institut study by Tabbert [301], analyzing a sample of 879 West German manufacturing firms, all of which had organized R & D activities, confirmed this finding of absolute concentration. Those with 10,000 or more employees, comprising 5.6 percent of the sample, accounted for 66.2 percent of total reported R & D spending; while those with under 1,000 employees comprised 63.3 percent of the sample but accounted for only 8.5 percent of the R&D expenditures. However, when Tabbert examined relative concentration within this sample, measured as R & D expenditures per employee, the relation between size and R & D disappeared. A further test of this sample showed that the elasticity of R & D/sales with respect to size was significantly greater than one in only 2 of 10 industry groups. A third study using data from West Germany collected by the Ifo-Institut, by Oppenländer [225], broke R & D activities into three phases: invention, innovation, and diffusion. He found that large firms, defined as those with over 5,000 employees, devoted greater percentages of sales and employment to invention than did the small and medium-sized ones. But in the years recently preceding 1975, the smaller firms were catching up. The principal advantage of large firms in invention, according to Oppenländer, was the capacity for long-range planning of their R & D activities. The small and medium firms, on the other hand, performed better than the large in innovation, or the conversion of their inventions into salable products and usable processes. Competition, Oppenländer concluded, is often an important force driving smaller firms to innovate promptly. The larger firms were superior in diffusion, for reasons discussed below in the section dealing with that phase of the innovation process.

Adams [1] found that R & D was less concentrated within the largest 300 firms in France than within the largest 300 in the United States, although average size among the 300 was much smaller in France. This, he pointed out, was inconsistent with the proposition that absolute firm size was important to R & D effort. Unlike the U.S. situation, the smaller size classes among the 300 top French firms accounted for higher proportions of R & D employment than of total employment in electrical equipment, chemicals, machinery and metals, and other manufacturing. The one exception was in France's aerospace sector.

Gannicott [80], noting problems of data limitation and looking only at firms which performed R & D, examined the effect of firm size on industrial R & D spending in 22 Australian industries, controlling for size of the industry, technological opportunity class, foreign ownership, and government R & D subsidies. He found that size was insignificant in an ordinary least squares regression but had a significant negative effect on R & D proportionate to sales in a two-stage regression. The latter regression also indicated the significance of a feedback effect in that firm size appeared dependent on R & D effort rather than the converse. Foreign ownership was positively related to R & D effort, but only in high and medium technology industries.

Smyth, Samuels, and Tzoannos [291] discovered that the number of patents obtained by a firm rose more than proportionately with company size in the British chemical industry, less than proportionately in that country's machine tool industry, and in an inverted "U" relationship in the electrical engineering and electronics group. Howe and McFetridge [108] found a variable for size "largely irrelevant" [p. 67] in explaining research intensity in the machinery sector of the Canadian economy and among foreign-owned firms in the chemical sector. Among the domestically owned chemical firms there appeared to be a threshold at about $80 million of annual sales. In the electrical sector, a cubic relationship emerged, with elasticities of R & D with respect to firm size greater than one in a middle range. Phlips [235] used Belgian survey data and found that the number of research workers grew more than proportionately up to a firm size of 7,000 employees, but that diminishing returns appeared to set in among a small sample of even larger firms. In a 1977 book, Jacquemin and de Jong [113] surveyed "the meagre stock of knowledge" [p. 155] on the European situation and concluded that it did not support the hypothesis that large scale was necessary for the efficient conduct of industrial R & D and for technological progress. In a survey of Japanese studies, Caves and Uekusa [38] reached a similar conclusion. In a 1982 book reviewing European data and studies, Freeman [72] emphasized the importance of a threshold size for survival in R & D intensive industries. Such minimal size, he observed, was required to provide technical services to customers and to imitate the innovations of others, even if a firm chose not to engage in original innovation. These threshold sizes, he continued, vary substantially among industries.

In the late 1970s and early 1980s new and more detailed data enriched a number of studies of heterogeneous aggregations of firms drawn from such broad categories as all U.S. manufacturing, or all private industry, without regard to specific market or product classifications. Soete [292] used data compiled by *Business Week* magazine on the R & D spending of over 700 of the largest U.S. corporations for 1975 and 1976 to challenge Scherer's [261] 1965 conclusion that there was no systematic relationship between size and R & D activity within the ranks of the largest firms. Using more detailed size breakdowns for the largest firms than had been available from NSF before 1972, Soete found that R & D effort, or overall expenditure as a percentage of sales, did increase with size, being particularly high for the six largest firms, each of which had more than 250,000 employees. But when the NSF's 17 industry groups were analyzed separately, no clear pattern of an increasing or decreasing relationship emerged. Soete interpreted his findings as refuting Scherer and as confirming the Schumpeterian hypothesis with regard to size. But his findings appear equally consistent with the 1967 summary of previous work with NSF data by Nelson, Peck, and Kalacheck [214], which noted that the apparent overall relationship between large size and R & D intensity is primarily an artifact of the association between high technology and large average firm size in a number of industries, and disappears when the analysis is done on an industry-by-industry basis.

The sensitivity of results to data assumptions in such across-the-board analyses is indicated by contrasting Soete's results with those from a slightly earlier analysis of the 1975 *Business Week* data that had been made by Scherer in 1977 [266]. Scherer adjusted the data by eliminating firms in the publishing, restaurant, and services categories and by incorporating the sales of Western Electric rather than those of its parent, A.T. & T. Soete adjusted by elimination of service companies and of oil companies whose sales figures he regarded as inflated by the oil crisis, before ranking firms by sales. Soete's and Scherer's findings are compared in Table II.

In another such broad study, but controlling for 21 industry groups, Bound, Cummins, Griliches, Hall, and Jaffe [24], utilized 1976 COMPUSTAT data on R & D spending by 1,492 enterprises

TABLE II

Concentration of sales and company-financed R & D, for large U.S. manufacturing corporations, 1975

Number of firms, ranked by sales	Scherer		Soete	
	% of sales	% of R & D	% of sales	% of R & D
First 8	25.3	24.5	24.7	30.9
First 20	38.1	38.1	35.8	43.4
First 50	55.4	55.6	52.2	59.6
First 100	70.7	70.3	67.5	72.7
All 644			100.0	100.0
All 679	100.0	100.0		

Sources: 268, p. 420; 292, p. 326.

in 1976. They discovered significant nonlinearities in the relationship estimated between the logarithms of R & D and sales: the elasticity of R & D intensity with respect to sales was 0.7 at sales of $1 million but 1.2 at sales of $1 billion. (The sample mean value for sales was $417.2 million.) "While a fairly linear relationship may exist for large firms," they observed [p. 34], "it clearly breaks down for smaller firms." Their results differed from those of earlier researchers such as Hamberg [99], Comanor [42], and Scherer [261], they suggested, because of the inclusion of smaller firms in their far more extensive data base. Most of the previous work, they pointed out, was based on samples of only larger firms such as those included among the *Fortune* 500.

Bound *et al.* believe that their "data cast strong doubt on the existence of any significant R & D threshold." [p. 50]. But this depends on one's concept of a "threshold effect." What the previous researchers criticized by Bound *et al.* have observed is that relatively few smaller firms perform R & D, and not that those small firms that do engage in R & D spend less relative to size than their larger competitors. Bound *et al.* have merely found that there is no observable threshold for a set of smaller firms that reported doing a material amount of R & D.

In the early 1980s a new data set became available through the U.S. Federal Trade Commission's Line of Business Program [315]. A line of business (LB) was defined as an individual firm's activity in any one of 261 manufacturing or 14 nonmanufacturing sectors. Under this program, several hundred of the largest U.S. manufacturing firms were required to report data on sales, expenses, profits, assets, and R & D, all broken down by LB.

Scherer combined LB data with an equally detailed and extensive set of patent data. For each of 196 industries, he calculated elasticities of R & D spending with respect to firm size (sales), using quadratic equations to ascertain whether the elasticity changed with size. He made similar calculations of patenting elasticities with respect to size of firm for 124 industry categories in which five or more firms received patents. His results are shown in Tables III and IV [272, pp. 233, 234].

The results, Scherer concluded [pp. 234–235], "tilt on the side of supporting the Schumpeterian hypothesis that size is conducive to vigorous conduct of R & D," but that "the evidence leans weakly

TABLE III
Elasticities of R & D spending with respect to size of firm

	Number of industries	Percentage
No significant departures from constant returns	140	71.4%
Increasing returns (elasticity greater than one):		
Throughout	29	
At higher sales levels	11	
	40	20.4
Diminishing returns (elasticity less than one throughout)	16	8.2

against the Schumpeterian conjecture that the largest sellers are especially fecund sources of patented inventions." These results were reconciled in a regression of patents on R & D spending which indicated diminishing returns, as reflected in Table V [p. 235].

In all, the preponderance of evidence from the newer studies indicates that economies of scale in industrial R & D, of both the firm and the research establishment, are in most cases exhausted well below the largest firm and research establishment sizes examined. The studies that have found a pervasive positive relationship between size and R & D intensity are those drawing on samples including companies of widely ranging sizes and with little or no control for industry effects. When one looks at samples such

TABLE IV
Elasticities of patenting with respect to size of firm

	Number of industries	Percentage
No significant departure from constant returns	91	73.4%
Increasing returns:		
Throughout	9	
At higher sales levels	5	
	14	11.3
Diminishing returns:		
Throughout	18	
At higher sales levels	1	
	19	15.3

TABLE V
Elasticities of patenting with respect to R & D spending

	Number of industries	Percentage
No significant departure from constant returns	74	59.7%
Increasing returns:		
Throughout	16	
At higher R & D levels	3	
	19	15.3
Diminishing returns:		
Throughout	30	
At higher R & D levels	1	
	31	25.0

as the *Fortune* 500 or the enterprises included in the FTC's Line of Business Program, any statistical relationship is tenuous at best. The Schumpeterian hypothesis relating innovation to size appears to hold up if interpreted as a threshold one, but does not imply that giant corporations are essential for vigorous R & D in most fields.

Perhaps the last word on this matter of scale belongs to Mansfield, as the thrust of his work and that of his associates has been to highlight differences among industries, and indeed among firms within industries, and thus to move beyond global generalizations. As he wrote in 1977 [185, p. 67]:

> In some industries, like steel, the biggest firms have carried out relatively few innovations; in other industries, like chemicals, the biggest firm seems to have performed very well. Moreover, the results vary, depending on the type of innovation. For example, the biggest chemical firm seems to have played a much more important role in product innovation than in pure process innovation. And the results can vary substantially, depending on whether one looks at innovations, development, or the basic concepts underlying innovations. This diversity is strikingly at odds with some of the simple generalizations found frequently in the literature.

In addition to emphasizing diversity, Mansfield's comment underscores the need to examine the various components of innovative activity and the varied settings in which it takes place, rather than merely a conglomeration labeled R & D. The contributions of Mansfield and others to this type of disaggregated analysis are reviewed later. But first we must survey the scattered findings on the hypothesized effects of other structural features on total R & D.

3.5. Concentration, conditions of entry, diversification, and product differentiability as determinants of R & D and innovation

For Schumpeter, both size and market power enhance a firm's ability and incentive to engage in R & D. Yet the number of empirical studies that have investigated the market power hypothesis since Scherer's 1965 analysis [261] is minuscule in comparison with those addressing the issue of size. A fundamental problem is that the slippery concept of market power cannot be measured directly. Thus, resort must be had to various proxies such as concentration, market share, profitability, and conditions of entry.

In their study of the food processing industries, Imel, Behr and Helmberger [110] found that company-funded R & D as a percentage of sales rose significantly with concentration. But in their later examination of the same industries, Culbertson and Mueller [48] identified a threshold of CR4 where the 4-firm concentration ratio was equal to 58 to 60 percent, beyond which there was no significant relationship between concentration and either R & D inputs or number of patents received relative to firm size.

Results qualifying or casting doubt on the hypothesis have been reported in five studies drawing on data from countries other than the United States. Tabbert [301], analyzing a sample of 879 West German R & D-performing manufacturing enterprises, reported only a weak confirmation of the relationship between concentration and R & D effort. He regressed both R & D/sales ratios and R & D spending per employee on 3- and 6-firm concentration ratios, including dummy variables for chemical, electrical, and "unprogressive" technological opportunity classes. The only significant positive relationship found was between R & D spending per employee and the 6-firm concentration ratio. Howe and McFetridge [108] found that concentration had no statistically perceptible effect on R & D spending in the industries comprising Canada's machinery and electrical sectors. In that country's chemical sector, there was a positive relationship between concentration and R & D intensity among foreign-owned firms, but a negative relationship among those that were domestically owned. Caves [34] compared ratios of R & D to sales in the United Kingdom and the United States and discovered that for those industries in which the British ratios were highest relative to their U.S. counterparts, seller concentration was lower in the United Kingdom. Both Jacquemin and de Jong [113] in their survey of western European nations, and Caves and Uekusa [38] in their survey of Japanese industrial studies, concluded that the available evidence did not support the conclusion that market dominance was required for high levels of R & D and rapid rates of technological progress.

In their 1977 book [185, p. 16], Mansfield and his colleagues noted that "far too little" work had been done on the effect of concentration on R & D, but that patterns were beginning to emerge from their studies and those of others. "[A] slight amount of concentration may promote more rapid invention and innovation . . . . But beyond a moderate amount of concentration, further increases in concentration do not seem to be associated with more rapid rates of technological advance."

Since Mansfield's 1977 assessment, the impact of concentration on R & D has been further investigated by Long [161], Scott [287], and Lunn and Martin [166], all of whom used the FTC's LB data.

Long conceived a model of oligopolistic interdependence in which firms' reactions to the innovative activities of rivals are indirect, in that they respond to one another's R & D-generated changes in output and quality. His regression results indicated that, after a number of other market structure variables are accounted for, concentration has a positive effect on cooperative or collusive behavior. One of these control variables, minimum efficient scale of operation (MES), turned out to have a negative effect, contrary to Long's initial hypothesis that MES would have the same positive effect on R & D cooperation as it has on profit. His unexpected result suggested the alternative hypothesis that higher MES, given concentration, implies greater cost differences among competitors, making cooperation or collusion more difficult.

Scott investigated the existence of an inverted "U" relationship between seller concentration and non-price competition, whether in R & D, our focus here, or in advertising. The theoretical work of Scherer [264], Kamien and Schwartz [131], Loury [162], and Futia [75] (reviewed in Section 2) had established a rationale for an inverted "U", and Scherer [263] had reported finding such a relationship in his 1967 empirical study (reviewed above in this section). But such a relationship could obtain because of variance in nonprice competition across industries or firms regardless of the existence or absence of oligopolistic collusion or recognition of mutual dependence.

To test for the effect of oligopolistic interdependence, Scott first ran a quadratic regression of R & D intensity on concentration for 3,388 LBs with no control variables and found a positive coefficient on the unsquared term and a negative coefficient on the squared term, with both being highly significant. However, when he introduced control variables for the 437 firms in the sample and for 20 SIC two-digit industry groups, the inverted "U" relationship vanished completely. These dummy variables were introduced to control for differences across firms in R & D value, cost, and opportunity for R & D in much greater detail than was possible in previous research using broader industry or technology classes. Although concentration varied considerably within the two-digit industries, it apparently had no intra-group impact on behavior.

This test, Scott pointed out, does not establish the absence of an inverted "U" relationship between collusion or recognition of mutual dependence on the one hand and R & D effort on the other. First, there are determinants other than concentration of an oligopolistic rationale. Also, his fixed-effects model with dummy variables for two-digit industry groups might not be the most appropriate way to control for the firm- and industry-specific differences with which he was concerned, since those differences may be reflected in the coefficients for each of the four-digit industry structural variables as well as in the two-digit level fixed effects. However, the model evidence suggests caution in interpreting the inverted "U" relationships found in previous models which, Scott concluded [p. 237], "may be artifacts of insufficient control."

Lunn and Martin [166] utilized LB data for 1975 to analyze the structural determinants of R & D spending per dollar of sales, including market share, concentration, firm size, diversification, profitability, and the advertising-to-sales ratio among their explanatory variables. Their results [p. 41] "more than anything else . . . demonstrate the complexity of industrial research and development." Comparison of these results with those of Scherer and Scott also demonstrates the effects of controlling for industry and firm effects. Lunn and Martin found that R & D/sales ratios rose with LB size, in contrast to the findings of both Scherer [273] and Scott [287, Table 10.6, p. 243], whose studies control for industry differences at a finer level of detail. Market share and the four-firm concentration ratio had positive effects on R & D effort in Lunn and Martin's study, but only in industries lacking rich technological opportunities, supporting Scherer's earlier finding [263]. Diversification did not appear to have a strong effect on R & D. But their study did not control for a complete set of firm effects, and thus confidence in the interpretation of the LB and industry level variables is lessened.

In Scott's work firm and industry effects together explain roughly 50 percent of the variance in LB R & D intensity, while seller concentration explains only 1.5 percent. Farber [64] has taken a novel approach to understanding some of the unexplained variance, hypothesizing that the more concentrated the markets in which those who purchase and use an innovation operate, the greater will be the rents generated by that innovation. Also, the more concentrated this buyers' market, the greater will be the ability of buying firms to retain these rents, *ceteris paribus*. The stimulus to the seller is its ability to appropriate a portion of this rent. This ability was hypothesized to increase with seller concentration.

In testing this hypothesis Farber found that R & D intensity declined as buyer concentration rose when the seller four-firm concentration ratio was below 15 percent, presumably reflecting the relative weakness of the seller's bargaining position, but rose at higher levels of seller concentration. When the buyer four-firm concentration ratio was less than 8 percent, seller concentration had a significant negative effect on R & D intensity, but a positive effect at higher levels. Farber concluded from his analysis of the effects of both seller and buyer concentration on R & D intensity that the positive effects of the former reported in previous studies may have been biased upward by failure to take into account the effect of the latter.

Grabowski and Baxter [91] reported both anecdotal and statistical evidence that in the U.S. chemical industry there is a leader-follower pattern in R & D expenditures. They also found a significant negative rank correlation between the coefficient of variation of research intensity and industry concentration across the U.S. manufacturing sector, a result suggesting that firms match their rivals' R & D spending more closely as concentration increases.

Conditions of entry have long been recognized as important

structural determinants of R & D. Two sorts of entry should be distinguished. First, there is entry through imitation of other firms' product innovations, or the adoption of processes innovated by others. Second, there is innovative entry into an existing market by firms from outside offering new products or new methods of making existing products. A number of studies of imitative entry are reviewed in Section 4. But since 1967, when Nelson, Peck, and Kalachek [214, p. 71] stated that the optimal structure for conceiving and introducing inventions must include "a rate of turnover among firms sufficient to accommodate enough new firms to prevent excessive traditionalism," there has been very little empirical work on the second aspect of entry, the movement into an industry by outside innovators.

Comanor [42] examined the role of scale economies relative to market size and absolute capital requirements, which he referred to as "technical entry barriers," in 21 broadly defined industries. He found that an inverted "U" relationship existed between these barriers and the incentive to perform R & D. He described the likely cause of this relationship as follows [p. 657]:

> Where technical barriers either effectively foreclose the entry of new firms or where they are quite low, research spending tends to be limited. Where barriers are moderate, however, and where prospects for some entry exist, research spending is greater. There is some indication, therefore, that the incentive for research is related to the goal of impeding entry, and that this objective exists only so long as entry has not been previously foreclosed. At the same time, however, the total absence of technical barriers also serves as a depressing factor.

Mansfield *et al.* [185] have found that conditions of entry are important since new firms and firms entering new markets are among the most significant contributors to technological change. Scale and capital barriers need not, they found, be substantial in high technology industries. "There is often," they concluded [p. 16], "a division of labor, smaller firms focusing on areas requiring sophistication and flexibility and catering to specialized needs, bigger firms focusing on areas requiring larger production, marketing, or technological resources." In a case study of the computer-aided design (CAD) industry, Kaplinsky [132] related similar factors to the industry's life cycle. The first stage of this life cycle was characterized by user development undertaken by large, technically advanced corporations; the second stage by entry of new, independent firms and rapid diffusion of technology; the third stage by growing concentration, largely through vertical and horizontal combination; and the fourth stage by offsetting tendencies toward further concentration of existing firms and the entry of new firms selling specialized CAD systems.

Nelson's hypothesis [207] that diversification stimulates R & D, especially basic research, has not fared much better in more recent empirical verification efforts than it did in Scherer's 1965 study [261], particularly when diversification is related to total R & D effort. The more recent studies have been plagued by product mix problems. Imel, Behr, and Helmberger [110] found that within the food processing industries company-funded R & D expenditures as a percentage of sales rose significantly with diversification. But firms with primary product classifications in industries doing below-average R & D, such as food processing, are more likely than not to move into industries characterized by higher levels of R & D effort when they diversify, thus increasing their average R & D effort even if their effort is less than the average of the industries entered. Grabowski's results [90] are anomolous in this regard: he found that diversification was a significant determinant of R & D intensity in the chemical and drug industries, but not in petroleum refining, although the first two industries were the more research intensive.

Using patent and R & D data disaggregated to the LB level, Scherer [274] correlated a summary index of the number and importance of each firm's LBs with residual errors from the industry regressions of R & D on sales and patents on sales. The correlations were small, divergent in sign, and not significantly different from zero. Scherer did, however, find a small positive and significant correlation between diversification and the residuals in the regression of patents on R & D, indicating a somewhat higher propensity to patent with greater diversification. Link [157] surveyed 329 firms in 11 broadly defined industrial groups, ascertaining the magnitudes of each firm's own R & D resources relative to technology purchased from others. He found that internal R & D contributed a greater proportion of a firm's overall technical advance, the larger the size of the firm, the more concentrated the firm's markets, and the greater its diversification. [See also 272.]

Comanor [40, 42] examined the effect of yet another structural variable, the extent to which products can be differentiated. For a large sample of R & D-performing firms, he found R & D intensity to be greater in industries producing consumer durables and investment goods than in those producing consumer nondurables and material inputs [42]. He interpreted this as supporting the view that product differentiability is a major element in the decision to undertake R & D.

3.6. The decomposition of R & D

Simple two-stage Schumpeterian models distinguishing only invention and innovation oversimplify the innovative process. As Scherer *et al.* pointed out in a 1958 study [277, pp. 334–35], "the innovation of complex new products or processes typically requires substantial outlays for development, design, engineering, testing, tooling, the construction of production facilities, market research, the establishment of distribution channels, advertising and promotion, and any number of other activities." The risk characteristics of the various stages of the innovation process differ considerably in both nature and magnitude, they observed.

In subsequent work [185], the Mansfield group explored the close ties between risk in industrial innovation and the specific stage of the process involved. A study of three firms' R & D programs found that the average probability of economic success of a project was 12 percent; but this was the product of three conditional probabilities—technical completion, commercialization, and economic success. The probability of achieving the technical objectives was around 60 percent. R & D typically accounted for well under one half of total innovation costs: tooling, manufacturing start-up, and marketing start-up costs usually ran two to three times as high as the costs of R & D. Development costs tended to rise as a proportion of total innovation costs with size of firm. Cost and time overruns appeared to be about as high in commercial R & D as in military, with average overrun ratios of 2.11 for cost and 2.95 for time in one major company studied.

In general, the best way to reduce industrial innovation risk is to proceed sequentially through the stages of applied research, formulation of specifications, prototype or pilot plant construction, and start-up activities. This sequential approach is, however, usually slower than an "overlapping stages" [187] approach, in which two or more stages are undertaken simultaneously. Thus, a project manager's decision as to the extent of schedule overlap usually poses a time–cost tradeoff of the sort central to Scherer's [264] theoretical model of rivalry and R & D intensity. (In one in-depth study of a single project, however, it appeared to Mansfield and his fellow investigators that an overlapping stages approach not only speeded up development time but would have allowed for earlier and less costly termination of the project if problems uncovered at any stage had made the project unworkable.) In a survey of 29 innovations, Mansfield *et al.* found a positive relationship between firm size and the extent of overlap. This was attributed to the greater ability of larger organizations, with larger and more specialized R & D, engineering, and marketing departments, to engage in a number of activities related to the same project simultaneously.

In 1980 [180] and 1981 [181] articles, Mansfield published the results of research on market structure and the composition of R & D expenditures, focusing on the more risky types of industrial research. In the first, he regressed the rate of increase of total factor productivity for 119 firms aggregated by industry on company-funded basic research and applied research expenditures as percentages of industry value added. Both of these independent variables had highly significant positive coefficients. Mansfield was concerned, however, that the basic research variable might be confounding the effects of longer-term R & D. When he added a variable for the percentage of firms in an industry that expected their 1958 R & D expenditures to pay off in no less than six years, the basic research coefficient declined and became statistically insignificant in some cases, while the payoff horizon variable was consistently significant.

The 1981 article extended the analysis to include firm size and concentration variables. Mansfield obtained data from 108 firms on the percentages of company-financed R & D spending allocated to basic research, projects lasting more than five years, projects aimed at entirely new products and processes, and projects with an estimated probability of success below 50 percent. The sample covered most manufacturing industries and consisted of firms accounting for approximately half the 1977 industrial R & D expenditures in the United States. Firm size was found to be associated with more than proportional increases in the fraction of company-funded R & D devoted to projects aimed at entirely new products and processes. There was no significant relationship between size and willingness to undertake projects with low probabilities of success. There was a negative and significant relationship between industry four-firm concentration ratios and the percentage of firms' R & D spending devoted to basic research. There were negative but insignificant relationships between concentration and the percentage of R & D spending devoted to long-term projects and to developing entirely new products and processes. The relationship between concentration and R & D devoted to risky projects was positive but insignificant.

The only other significant contributor to this line of investigation is Link [153, 154, 156]. Using questionnaire responses from 174 of *Fortune*'s 1,000 largest U.S. industrial corporations, Link [154] fitted cubic regressions of R & D expenditures on firm size for total R & D, basic research, applied research, and development. In all four regressions, the first order term was positive, the squared term was negative, and the cubic term positive, indicating that R & D intensity decreased with size throughout a middle range of firm sizes, but then increased with size among the largest firms. Since there were few very large firms in his sample, Link interpreted his results as consistent with those of Worley [339], Hamberg [99], Comanor [42], and Scherer [261]. But when he broke his sample down and ran separate regressions for each of eleven industry groups, the uniformity of pattern and most of the statistical significance disappeared—a result consistent with the earlier Nelson–Peck–Kalachek [214] interpretation of National Science Foundation data.

With a larger sample of 275 firms [153, 156], Link examined the composition of R & D effort. Among his findings are the following. Diversification, while not exerting a significant influence on overall R & D intensity, did appear to have a significant positive effect on the proportion of R & D funds devoted to basic research. This result supports Nelson's [207] diversification hypothesis, since it is basic research which is most likely to lead to the broadest range of exploitable opportunities. Concentration was negatively related to basic research allocations and positively related to the proportion of R & D funds spent on development, contrary to Link's initial hypothesis that profitability should favor relatively risky allocations to basic research, but consistent with the observation of Jewkes, Sawers, and Stillerman [116] that firms with market power enjoy an advantage in introducing new products. A variable for high technological opportunity was positively correlated with overall R & D intensity; but contrary to expectations, high opportunity appeared to favor development over basic research. Link found that none of the structural variables exerted a significant influence on the division between product and process R & D. Consistent with product and industry life-cycle models, R & D was more product-oriented in the high opportunity industries. Control of a corporation by an identifiable ownership group, as contrasted to managerial control, also appeared to favor the allocation of funds to basic research. Link pointed out that this result is consistent with the widely accepted hypothesis that manager-controlled firms tend to be more risk averse than those controlled by their owners, since managers do not share fully in the benefits of successful risk taking. According to his interpretation, such risk aversion extends to the typically very small fraction of R & D expenditures devoted to basic research.

Link's analysis of the effects of corporate control is consistent with the results of a study by McEachern and Romeo [193] using a more detailed breakdown of control forms; but the explanatory hypotheses in the two studies are widely divergent. McEachern and Romeo classified control into three categories—outside owner, owner-managed, and manager-controlled. With a sample of 40 firms drawn from three industries, they found that enterprises controlled by an outside stockholder interest were more R & D-intensive than either the owner-managed or manager-controlled firms, *ceteris paribus*. Their explanation was that since outside owners are less well informed than those actively involved in management, whether owners or not, they face greater uncertainty and thus tend to favor less risky business strategies. Risk aversion of this sort, however, as interpreted by McEachern and Romeo, calls for greater rather than less R & D intensity, since R & D is necessary to defend market positions.

Link and Lunn [159] pointed out that high market share enhances the appropriability of results from process-oriented R & D, since the greater the share a firm has in some market, the greater the internal benefit it enjoys from improved production processes. The theoretical relationship between market share and the appropriability of product-oriented R & D is weaker, they asserted, since the return to an innovation can be realized by licensing as well as internal production, and licensed process innovations are more difficult to protect with patents than are product innovations. The hypothesis was tested by relating rates of return to process- and product-related R & D expenditures to levels of industry concentration for the 275 firms in Link's sample. As posited, returns to process R & D did rise with concentration, while the returns to product R & D were not significantly related to concentration.

In all, as the underlying theory has advanced and as data sources have become richer, a growing body of empirical work has demonstrated that the relationships running from structure to innovation through R & D effort are complex. One of Schumpeter's original hypotheses, asserting simply that size and market power promote innovation, has been qualified and extended to include other aspects of structure. But the underlying vision, that market structure is an important determinant of technological progress, continues to attract industrial organization scholars and to motivate much empirical economic research.

3.7. Feedback hypotheses

The "perennial gale of creative destruction," or the dynamic competitive process in which "the new commodity, the new technology" threatens the "foundations" and "very lives" of existing firms, was integral to Schumpeter's vision of the capitalist process. "The problem that is usually being visualized," he wrote [283, p. 84], "is how capitalism administers existing structures, whereas the relevant problem is how it creates and destroys them." From the earliest statistical analyses of the Schumpeterian hypothesis, a few writers such as Phillips [231] and Horowitz [107] called attention to this long-run "feedback" feature of Schumpeter's system. In Mansfield's 1968 book [179], studies of the steel and petroleum industries revealed that successful innovators grew much more rapidly than previously comparable firms for a five to ten year post-innovation period. Successful innovation in his sample raised annual growth rates by 4 to 13 percent, with the impact being much greater for small than large firm growth.

In a 1966 article [232] and a 1971 book [233], Phillips returned to this theme, now the central point of his analyses. In the article, Phillips argued that one determinant of industry structure is the extent to which the industry's underlying science base facilitates product change and differentiation. Drawing on NSF data for company size classes within 11 industry groups and a "subjective evaluation" of the science-based potential for product change and differentiation in each group, Phillips conducted a "crude empirical test" [p. 305], concluding [p. 307] that "Where science permits early product change and differentiation, the market process tends over time to cause the scale of surviving firms to be large and concentration to be high." In his 1971 book, Phillips examined the history of the commercial aircraft industry, stressing that the underlying technology unfolded primarily from exogenous sources, and that neither size nor market power explained the relative R & D performances of the industry's firms. However, relative success in innovation was the primary cause of the growth of some firms and the decline or demise of others, and hence of growing concentration.

Branch [26, 27] hypothesized and tested for a two-way causal relationship: successful R & D leads to increased sales growth and profit, and both growth and profit stimulate additional R & D. In a distributed lag analysis using patent counts as indicia of R & D, he found strong support for the hypothesis that successful R & D does indeed lead to increased profits (although not necessarily increased rates of profit) and more rapid sales growth. His tests of the hypothesis that higher profit leads to greater R & D yielded mixed results but "some support" [27, p. 1010].

Branch's findings were corroborated and extended in subsequent studies by Grabowski and Mueller [92] and Ravenscraft and Scherer [239]. Rather than using patents, Grabowski and Mueller treated a firm's R & D outlays as capital expenditures, increasing the firm's asset base but depreciating over time. When both R & D and advertising were so capitalized, the rate of return on R & D capital in research-intensive industries was found to be significantly above rates of return available from alternative investments. The rate of return on capitalized R & D was higher in the more concentrated industries, but the coefficient on a concentration-research interaction variable was negative and highly significant. Grabowski and

Mueller [p. 338] interpreted this result as indicating "that the negative effect of concentration on profitability is confined to the research intensive industries in our sample, which is consistent with the R & D rivalry hypothesis." That is, in highly concentrated industries that are research intensive, R & D competition may replace price competition as a force holding profit down—a gentle version of the creative gale.

Ravenscraft and Scherer investigated the distributed lag structure of returns to R & D, using the Strategic Planning Institute's PIMS (profit impact of market strategy) data for the 1970's, and a form free distributed lag estimation technique. They found "strong evidence" (p. 619) of a roughly bell-shaped lag structure, with a four to six year mean lag. When structural variables were added to the estimating equation, most of the effect of R & D on profit was captured by interaction variables, yielding the "somewhat puzzling" [p. 618] result that the greatest impact appeared to be "in markets that are relatively mature, technologically undynamic, and consumer-goods oriented (which tends to coincide with low technological dynamism)." Ravenscraft and Scherer speculated that a possible explanation was that R & D-based competition had become so intense in the more technologically dynamic markets by the 1970s that profit opportunities had declined markedly.

Scherer [270, 271] used the U.S. Federal Trade Commission's Line of Business data, along with data he had developed on industries of origin and use of patents, to investigate the association between long-run productivity growth and concentration. Most industrial R & D is aimed at new products, with process R & D accounting for only 24.6 percent of the company-financed total in the 1974 LB sample. On the same line of reasoning as that subsequently followed by Link and Lunn [159], Scherer posited that the larger a firm's market share, the larger should be its share of the cost saving resulting from a process innovation, and hence the greater its incentive to engage in process R & D. To test the hypothesis, Scherer regressed the annual percentage change in real output per hour of work against weighted-average seller concentration ratios and growth in capital stock for 87 industry groups. The effect of concentration was positive and significant. But when two variables measuring 1974 product- and process-oriented R & D as percentages of sales were added to the regressions, concentration became insignificant. The coefficients on both R & D variables were positive, but only that for product-oriented R & D was significant. The underlying economic phenomenon behind the behavior of the concentration variable, as Scherer interpreted it [271, p. 224], is a "complex set of relationships" in which "concentration leads to greater R & D intensity, which in turn leads to faster measured productivity growth."

In a 1983 study, Mansfield [183] examined whether technological changes associated with process innovations in the twentieth century have generally tended to be scale-diminishing, as asserted by Blair [21], or scale-augmenting; and whether the introduction of new products has tended to retard or promote concentration. Mansfield sampled major process innovations in the chemical, petroleum, and steel industries, and major product innovations in these three plus the drug industry. He further obtained evaluations of these innovations' scale and concentration effects from high-level engineers in 34 firms. In the three industries for which he had data, Mansfield found that scale-increasing process innovations clearly predominated over scale-decreasing ones. (See also Scherer *et al.* [276, pp. 82–83], which found that changes in technology had led to "radical increases" in minimum optimal scale of plant in steel and cement from the 1950s to 1965, and more gradual rises in paints, refrigerators, brewing, and battery manufacture).

Among the product innovations studied by Mansfield, on the other hand, those judged to have decreased concentration comprised a "substantial portion" [p. 207] of the total. In the petroleum and steel industries, the concentration-increasing product innovations greatly outnumbered the concentration-decreasing ones. But in the chemical industry, there were almost as many concentration-decreasing product innovations as concentration-increasing ones; and in the drug industry the concentration-decreasing product innovations outnumbered the concentration-increasing ones. Mansfield concluded that innovation often reduces concentration because the innovators are new entrants to the relevant market (frequently invaders from other markets) or relatively small firms.

Mukhopadhyay [202] examined changes in the four- and eight-firm concentration ratios for U.S. industries from 1963 to 1977, finding that high and medium levels of research intensity across 336 industries tended to be associated with falling concentration.

Further, research intensity was positively related to rates of entry. Mukhopadhay concluded that his statistical results failed to support the concentration-increasing effects of high technological opportunity depicted in Nelson's and Winter's simulation models [217, 219] because Nelson and Winter did not allow for entry. "The main reason why concentration ratios, on the average, went down in the technologically progressive industries in the U.S.A.," according to Mukhopadhyay [p. 148], "seems to be that the net rate of entry was much higher in those industries." Mukhopadhyay's regressions distinguished only among high, medium, and low R & D intensity, however, and thus did not test for the significance of the distinction between exogenous and endogenous sources of technology that is crucial in the Nelson–Winter model and in Phillips' [233] empirical study.

Feedback from R & D and innovation may impact on elements of structure other than firm size and concentration. MacDonald [167] has examined the effects of R & D on diversification. Such effects might exist, he pointed out, because R & D in the "destination" industry, or that diversified into, might make firms in that industry attractive to "origin" or diversifying firms, particularly if the latter could provide managerial, financial, and marketing skills lacking in some of the former. Further, firms with substantial R & D experience and skills may direct their diversification towards R & D-intensive industries in which their technological capabilities are most valuable. Employing both U.S. Census and LB data for 67 industries, MacDonald found that R & D intensity in both origin and destination industries was positively associated with diversification. Differences between the R & D intensities of two industries had a significant negative effect on diversification from one to the other. Reinforcing Scherer's [261] point that a spurious relationship running from diversification to R & D may appear when firms in low R & D industries diversify into those with higher R & D intensities, MacDonald's analysis indicated that diversifying firms are equally likely to enter industries with similar or higher R & D intensities than their own, but not those with lower. Concentration in the destination industry, MacDonald found, posed a barrier to entry that inhibited diversification into it; while concentration in the origin industry promoted outbound diversification.

Studies of the feedback from innovation to industry structure have called attention to the problem of relating hypothesized causality to the results of regression analysis. This problem is compounded in working with the Line of Business file, as rich as it otherwise is, because of its very short time coverage. It would not be possible, for example, to replicate the sort of time lags used by Branch. An alternative approach is application of simultaneous equation models in which both structural variables of interest and variables measuring the innovative activity under study are treated as endogenous.

Neumann, Böbel and Haid [221] estimated a simultaneous equation model in which R & D effort, technical progress, firm growth, firm size, and industry concentration were all endogenous variables. Their data covered 283 West German manufacturing firms from 1965 to 1977. Technical progress was measured as the undeflated rate of growth of value added per worker, controlled for growth of the capital/labour ratio.

Among their findings are the following. Technical progress was found to rise with firm growth and R & D intensity but decline with concentration and firm size. Size stimulated R & D intensity, while concentration dampened it. Growth was a positive function of technical progress, size, and concentration. Thus, both firm size and concentration were found to have adverse direct effects on technical progress. But size had a favorable indirect effect on technical progress through its direct effect on R & D intensity, while concentration had a similarly favorable indirect effect through firms' growth rates.

Echoing Jewkes, Sawers and Stillerman [116], Neumann, Böbel, and Haid speculated [p. 135] that "larger firms and firms in concentrated industries acquire smaller firms in order to exploit the innovative potential originated in these firms." Thus, they concluded [p. 138], "we tentatively envisage a picture of a modern industrial economy where large and small firms assume complementary roles. Smaller firms, particularly those in competitive industries, enjoy a comparative advantage in developing new technical knowledge. On the other hand, large firms, disadvantaged at inventive activity, do have advantages at utilizing mass production techniques to bring to industrial maturity ideas which they had to buy by the acquisition of smaller firms."

Lunn [165] made use of a system of equations in which concentration, advertising and both product and process patenting were all endogenous, to examine differences in the determinants and effects of process- and product-oriented R & D. His analysis of the large firms included in the LB data set indicated that concentration was a significant positive determinant of the extent of process patenting in industries facing lower technological opportunities but not in those with higher opportunities, supporting the earlier findings of Scherer [271, 272]. But concentration was not a statistically significant determinant of product patenting, at least among these large firms. Greater process patenting appeared to lead to increases in concentration, but the coefficient on the product patenting variable in the concentration equation was not significantly different from zero.

The most ambitious and theoretically inclusive empirically specified simultaneous equation model is that of Levin and Reiss [150]. Adapted from Dasgupta and Stiglitz [49], this model treats industry concentration and the intensity of both advertising and R & D as endogenous and as determined by more fundamental forces of demand, technological opportunity, and appropriability. The empirical results were inconclusive. Data limitations required Levin and Reiss to work at a highly aggregated level with 20 broadly defined industry classes. One resulting problem was the inability to develop a satisfactory variable for industry concentration. The analysis suffered even more from a conceptual drawback. As Levin and Reiss conceded, their simultaneous equation framework implies static equilibrium. "[A] model of Schumpeterian competition without dynamics, without transient monopoly, without innovators and imitators is, at best, only part of the story," they concluded [p. 202]. "Much remains to be done."

3.8. The technological environment

According to E. S. Mason [191, p. 69], who first proposed the structure-conduct-performance approach to industrial organization, "The structure of a seller's market, then, includes all those considerations which he takes into account in determining his business policies and practices." For R & D and the pace of innovation the relevant structural influences include features of the underlying technological environment as well as the more traditional firm and market characteristics.

Case studies led Mansfield [178] to conclude that anticipated profitability is a major factor in firms' decisions to engage in R & D. But in an in-depth study of one active R & D performer, expected profit explained only about half the observed allocation of funds. Executives and scientists suggested in interviews that the other principal determinants were the scientific and professional goals of the researchers, intrafirm politics, changes made in initial cost and revenue estimates by multi-level reviewing bodies, a tendency to concentrate on shorter-term projects, and, most important, differences in the abilities of the researchers and their supervisors to promote their proposals.

Two elemental features of the technological environment that have been recognized as having important effects on industrial R & D are opportunity and appropriability. The opportunity for R & D-based innovations depends on the state of knowledge in relevant fields of science and technology. Appropriability refers to the ability of the innovating firm to capture the social benefits from its innovation as private gain. Appropriability is determined by such things as initial market share, the ability to practice price discrimination, the extent of effective patent protection, practicability of licensing, ability to preserve secrecy, feasibility of reverse engineering by rivals, and ability of an imitator to penetrate an innovator's market.

Several studies discussed above recognized the need to take account of differences in technological opportunity. Scherer's pioneering 1965 and 1967 studies [261, 263] grouped industries into three or four technology classes designed to reflect these differences. Lunn and Martin [166] confirmed Scherer's results in a finding that concentration had a significant effect on R & D effort only in those industries dichotomously classified as having low rather than high technological opportunities. Link [154] found that much of a previously observed effect of size on R & D effort was eliminated by classifying a sample of 174 firms into 11 industry groups. In Scott's [287] fixed effects model, taking account of both industry and firm effects, the inverted "U" relationship between concentration and R & D intensity vanished.

Four more recent studies have built on earlier contributions, using a number of variables to depict the underlying technological environment in more detail than their predecessors.

Wilson [336] incorporated Comanor's [42] insight that the opportunity for new product innovation depends upon the extent to which the basic product line is amenable to differentiation in a model with two dimensions of technological opportunity—"the richness of opportunities . . . arising from exogenous advances in science and technology," and "the ease with which physical characteristics of the product can be altered. In particular, as the complexity of a product's configuration options increases, more variations of this product can be produced with a given amount of effort." [p. 171]. He referred to these two dimensions as "opportunity" and "complexity" respectively. Fifty industries analyzed were divided into three opportunity groups, high, medium, and low. Each industry's product complexity was scored from 1 to 4, depending upon the number and complexity of configuration options. Both high opportunity and complexity had significant and positive effects on R & D/sales ratios for 350 large firms. The effect of low opportunity was negative and significant as hypothesized. Size of firm had a positive but not statistically significant effect, while concentration had a negative effect significant only at the 10 percent level.

Link and Long [158] followed Wilson's approach in an analysis of the determinants of basic research, including dummy variables for high and low opportunity and for complexity as well as diversification. For a sample of 250 manufacturing firms, they found that diversification was a positive and significant determinant of basic research expenditure/sales ratios, as was high technological opportunity. The coefficient on industry concentration was positive but not significant.

Shrieves [289] attacked the problem through factor analysis, deriving five technological and two product market factors from scientific specialist employment and sales mix data for 411 companies. The technological factors were interpreted to represent 1) life sciences, 2) electronics and aerospace, 3) process orientation in production technology, 4) mechanical and electromechanical, and 5) chemical technology orientation. The product-market factors were interpreted to represent durable goods and the industry's relative involvement in producing materials used by other industries. An important by-product of Shrieves' market structure analysis was evidence on the effects of the technological and product-market factors. The life sciences technological factor was positively and significantly related to R & D effort, while the mechanical and electromechanical factor was negatively and significantly related. The relationships between R & D effort and the other three technological factors were negative but weak. Firms heavily involved in manufacture of material inputs and durable goods appeared to perform more R & D, *ceteris paribus,* than those primarily engaged in consumer goods production. When Shrieves' sample was partitioned by product market characteristics, seller concentration was found to have a negative effect on R & D performance by producers of specialized durable equipment, but a positive one on producers of nonspecialized producers' durable goods, materials, and consumer goods. The concentration effect was positive and significant for firms whose technologies were mainly in life sciences and chemistry, and negative but insignificant for those that drew their technologies primarily from the electronics, aerospace, mechanical and electromechanical fields. Shrieves concluded that concentration played an ambiguous role in determining R & D performance, depending primarily on types of products and markets.

Levin, Cohen, and Mowery [148] combined the FTC's line of business data with data from a 1984 survey carried out by researchers at Yale University [149]. Surveyed executives in 130 industries were asked to scale the rate at which they introduced innovations in each industry their firm occupied. The responses were used to construct a measure of innovation. Research intensity was measured as the ratio of company financed R & D expenditures to sales. When these measures of R & D output and input were regressed on concentration and its square, Levin *et al.* obtained statistically significant inverted "U" relationships in both cases. Controlling for two-digit industry group effects reduced the statistical significance of the results, but did not change them. In every case, their inverted "U" peaked at four-firm concentration ratios between 0.5 and 0.6—values consistent with those reported in Scherer's 1967 study [263]. Levin *et al.* then added eight variables, constructed from responses to the Yale survey, to measure technological opportunity and appropriability. Six opportunity variables reflected respondents' evaluations of the importance of the scientific base; exogenous contributions to the industry's technical knowledge from raw material and equipment suppliers, product users, and government agencies and research labs; and maturity of the industry's installed technology as reflected in the average age of property, plant, and equipment. Two appropriability variables scaled the effectiveness of appropriation mechanisms such as patents, secrecy, and lead time and the ease of imitation (measured as the average number of months required to duplicate a major patented product). In both the R & D intensity and innovation equations, the concentration coefficient remained positive, and that on its square negative, when these technological environment variables were included. But both the magnitudes of the coefficients and the *t*-statistics reflecting their significance all fell "by an order of magnitude." [p. 23]. The only concentration term retaining statistical significance at the 0.10 level was the unsquared variable in the innovation equation. Assessing the role of the technological environment variables, Levin *et al.* observed [p. 23]:

> There are no anomalous signs; the survey [technological environment] variables as a whole and the opportunity measures in particular are highly significant. Specifically, R & D spending appears to be encouraged in youthful industries where a strong science base is present and where the government makes a substantial contribution to technological knowledge.

The most important common feature of the few R & D and innovation analyses that have sought to control for the underlying technological environment is a dramatic reduction in the observed impact of the Schumpeterian size and market power variables. Furthermore, the studies extend Scherer's finding that the effects of the Schumpeterian variables are greatest in industries whose technological environment is less conducive to innovative activity and in which the R & D effort is therefore less intense. The implication would seem to be that firm and industry structural effects may well exist but, as suggested by theoretical contributions reviewed in Section 2, may be modified and sometimes obscured by strong technological determinants. But none of the studies finding significant Schumpeterian structural effects has controlled convincingly for firm and industry effects.

3.9. From structure to performance: private and social returns to innovation

The divergence between private and social returns to innovation has long been recognized as a possible source of market failure, with potentially severe consequences for economic performance. Mansfield and his colleagues [185, 186] estimated the magnitudes of this divergence for 17 innovations and, more to the point of this essay, sought to identify structural determinants of the observed differences. The average social rate of return on total innovative outlays was 56 percent, while the private rate of return averaged 25 percent. On 4 of the 17 innovations, however, the private rate of return exceeded the social rate. In those 4 cases, innovators were able to divert substantial amounts of business from their competitors.

The social rates of return on some "mundane" innovations were extremely high—307 percent on a sewing thread and 209 percent on a household cleaner. "Without denying the importance of 'high technology' industries," the authors commented [185, p. 189], "one is led to wonder whether there may not be a tendency in some quarters to underestimate the returns available from more R and D and related innovative activities in the relatively 'low technology' industries."

Mansfield *et al.* identified two factors that might affect the gap between private and social benefits: 1) the degree of competition determines the proportion of total social benefits the innovator can appropriate; and 2) an innovation stimulates others to incur costs in "innovating around" the original discovery.

Regression analysis showed a greater positive difference between social and private returns for product than for process innovations, consistent with the hypothesis that secrecy was easier to maintain for the latter. The difference was also greater for major innovations than for minor ones, supporting a hypothesis that major innovations are likely to be imitated more rapidly. It made no significant difference whether an innovation was patented, but the difference between social and private returns was significantly smaller, the greater the minimum cost of legal (i.e., patent-circumventing) imitation. In all, the authors concluded [185, p. 188], their analysis revealed "the key role of competition in driving a wedge between the private and social returns from innovation."

3.10. Summary and assessment

Over four decades have passed since the first edition of Schumpeter's *Capitalism, Socialism, and Democracy* appeared. Our knowledge of the statistical interrelationships between market structure and technological progress has expanded far beyond Schumpeter's impressionistic empiricism. Yet his vision still challenges empirical researchers as well as theorists.

Although the firm-size threshold concept attributed to Schumpeter by Markham seems well verified and pervasive, it has been equally well demonstrated that among the larger enterprises in individual industries the causal relationships running from firm size to R & D effort and innovative output are, if identifiable at all, weak. In specifications without full control for appropriability and opportunity differences, there appears to be some positive relationship between increased industry concentration and innovative activity at lower levels of concentration. But in Mansfield's words [185, p. 16], "beyond a moderate amount of concentration, further increases in concentration do not seem to be associated with more rapid rates of technological advance." Indeed, there is some evidence, although disputed and subject to question, that high levels of concentration tend to dampen R & D.

Both the requisite firm size threshold and the degree of market power most conducive to R & D may vary across and within industries. Some types of R & D may be most efficiently carried out by small, flexible organizations, while others may require large-scale efforts. If complementary R & D is pursued within an industry, and if the different types of R & D are best performed by firms of varying sizes and market positions, there may be a rationale for Schumpeter's large monopolistic firms not reflected in regressions analyzing *industrywide* statistics on size, concentration, R & D effort, and innovative output.

New firms, or established firms entering a new market through innovation, appear to have made disproportionately large innovative contributions. This suggests that greater attention should be paid to the analysis of relationships among conditions of entry, turnover of firms, and the introduction of new technology. Feedback phenomena are of particular significance here, since changes in industry technology will have major effects on both natural and artificial barriers to entry.

Despite widespread recognition that the modern large corporation is typically diversified, empirical studies have not yet dealt adequately with the hypothesis that diversification promotes R & D, and especially basic research. A diversified company's R & D in a particular product line may be influenced not only by the number of other industries in which it operates, but also by the technical characteristics of its other activities. For example, one firm may do more R & D related to its activities in electrical motors and generators than does a second in part because the first is also involved in such high-technology activities as aircraft and semiconductors while the second, although equally diversified, is engaged in meat packing and household furniture manufacture. That is, the first firm is, in a broad sense, more technologically oriented, even though the second may enjoy spillovers that lead it to do above average R & D in its low-technology activities. More detailed analysis of these firm-specific effects, including intra-firm spillover, seems required for adequate empirical testing of the diversification hypothesis.

The most significant change over time in the focus of the empirical literature appears to be the greater attention given to causal links running from innovation to structure. Indeed, this longer-run feedback effect, or process of creative destruction, may well prove to be the most important phenomenon in the Schumpeterian schema. Modeling and testing the relevant hypotheses in a dynamic process with industry structure, firms' R & D effort, and innovation all endogenous pose some of the greatest challenges for future work.

Equally promising and difficult work remains to be done on the impact of the underlying technological environment, elements of which evidently modify and at times reverse the direction of firm and industry structural effects.

Finally, no empirical study has yet addressed the issue of optimality of the R & D investment undertaken. Exploration across industries of the impact of market structure on the divergence of actual R & D investment from the socially optimal level remains to be done.

4. DIFFUSION BY DISSEMINATION AND IMITATION

4.1. Some basic distinctions

The effect of technological change on economic welfare depends ultimately upon the degree to which innovations are diffused, or made available to potential producers and users. This diffusion process, and the structural context in which it occurs, pose difficult issues for the normative evaluation of performance. At the most fundamental level, once an innovation has been carried out, society benefits from the widest and freest possible access to it (barring external diseconomies in its application). But the prospect of unlimited access may retard the flow of future innovations by reducing would-be innovators' incentives.

Certain basic distinctions need to be made at the outset. First, an innovation can originate at either the producing or using level, and it is necessary to identify at which of these levels the diffusion is being analyzed. An innovation will spread among users—e.g., various railroads adopted the diesel locomotive at diverse times. It will also diffuse among producers—e.g., the manufacturers of railway equipment phased out steam locomotive production and turned to producing diesels with varying alacrity.

Second, the rate and extent of diffusion have been measured in two different ways. Some studies have used the number of potential producing or using firms that have adopted the innovation, regardless of size or market share, as the index of diffusion [88, 185]. Others have been concerned with the percentage of total industry output or purchases—or the degree of market penetration—achieved by the innovation, regardless of the number of firms involved [218].

Third, diffusion involves both the initial adoption of a new technology by firms, or *interfirm* diffusion, and the subsequent *intrafirm* diffusion of the technology as any given firm's old machines and facilities are replaced.

Finally, and perhaps most significantly for a study of the links between industry structure and technological change, interfirm diffusion may result from deliberate attempts of the innovating firm to encourage adoption, or at least occur with its acquiescence; or it may come from competitive imitation of the original new process or product. The term "imitation" is well established in the literature as denoting diffusion by actors other than the innovator, and without its permission or approval. We follow Hirshleifer [106] and use the word "dissemination" for diffusion initiated or encouraged by the innovator, to distinguish it from imitation. Such dissemination may be a crucial feature of technological performance. Culbertson and Mueller [48], for example, found that U.S. firms in other industries, foreign firms, and individual inventors played such a preponderant role in originating innovations used in the U.S. food processing industries that the effects of structural determinants of R & D within these industries had only insignificant implications for appropriate public policies toward these industries.

4.2. Dissemination and the market for knowledge

Perhaps the most fundamental concept underlying the analysis of dissemination is the abstract one of a market for pure disembodied knowledge [7, 106, 168]. Severe, even crippling, sources of market failure have been identified when knowledge, in and of itself, is viewed as the commodity transferred or diffused in a process of voluntary exchange. If such abstract knowledge is envisaged as salable, its marginal cost of production approximates zero. Discovering or producing pure, disembodied knowledge may be quite costly. But once a unit has been produced and is available to its discoverer, it can be reproduced, or divulged to others, at little or no cost. I.e., the costs of producing pure knowledge are fixed, and there are negligible variable costs involved in expanding output, when this output is measured as the number of persons to whom the knowledge has been revealed.

Closely related to the idea of zero marginal production cost is that marginal user cost is also zero. The availability to one person of a unit of knowledge is in no way diminished by supplying such units to others. In this sense, knowledge, once in being, is an inexhaustible common resource.

The implication of zero marginal production and social user cost is that, by standard criteria, the contribution to welfare of pure disembodied knowledge is maximized when its price is zero. That is, it should be made freely available to all. In Arrow's words [7, p. 617], "In a free-enterprise economy, inventive activity is supported by using the invention to create property rights; precisely to the extent that it is successful, there is an underutilization of the information." But of course, without some way of providing returns to the innovator, the information would not be there to underutilize.

There is a paradox in the market for knowledge. Markets are presumed to work efficiently only if both buyers and sellers have complete and accurate information on the commodities being traded. But by definition, this necessary condition for efficiency is violated, since buyers of knowledge do not know what they are acquiring, nor what its worth to them will be, until after they have bought it [7]. For if they had sufficient knowledge, they would not have to acquire it.

Finally, the market for knowledge is often viewed as an imperfect one, with the seller enjoying substantial market power *vis-à-vis* buyers. Large, technically sophisticated innovators may face potential buyers who are poorly informed and in weak bargaining positions [35, 36, 60, 103, 188, 305, 306]. Alternatively, the discoverer of a new unit of knowledge (such as an independent scientist) may not be in a strong position to exploit it, and thus the preponderance of market power may lie with large enterprises which are the main potential customers of a new technology [116, 195, 200, 221, 256, 312].

4.3. Methods of and motives for dissemination

The concept of a market for pure disembodied knowledge with zero marginal cost is a severe, though illuminating, abstraction. Knowledge, at least as applied to technology, is more realistically viewed as incapable of being disseminated in its pure form. For one thing, knowledge is ultimately embodied in the materials, machinery, products, and processes that comprise an innovation. For another, it is embedded in records of various sorts and in the minds of individuals.

The accurate and complete transfer of embodied technology, typically through sale of a new product, may require instruction manuals, verbal and written explanations, and the know-how acquired only through operating experience. Sellers may need the capacity to provide proper repair and maintenance service, as well as to stock an adequate inventory of replacement parts. As Rubenstein [254, p. 395] observed, "Few transfers of technology beyond simple provisions of new parts or equipment embodying changes can be completed by 'mail' or by 'arms length' exchanges. They generally require 'hands on' instruction and cooperation in installation, start-up, breaking in, adapting, improving training for use and maintenance, and going through the other activities that are required for effective and 'full' transfer of technology."

The learning curve phenomenon, or the decline in costs associated with cumulated output or production experience, may retard diffusion of embodied technology. Sources of such cost reduction include workers learning the skills involved in operating with a new technology; elimination of "bugs" or start-up problems; managerial experience with layout, work flow, and avoidance of material waste; use of appropriate materials; and establishment of good commercial relations with reliable sources of supply including, in some cases, working with vendors to develop their capabilities to supply new items. Lower costs attainable only through experience may put those who adopt the technology later at a serious enough competitive disadvantage to retard dissemination in some cases, and imitation in others. Several of those who have discussed the learning curve as a barrier to diffusion have noted that more research needs to be done on the extent and strength of the phenomenon across various industries and technologies and, perhaps more important, the extent to which experience can be transmitted from one firm to another [23, 47, 88, 254].

Where embedded knowledge is complex, and diffusion takes the form of technology transfer, errors and misunderstandings are likely to occur. The transfer of technical information is rarely, if ever, costless; and it may be risky as well [188, 254, 305, 306].

Those seeking to transfer embedded technology may fail in the effort, Rubenstein notes, for lack of the capacity to write accurate specifications or to give needed ongoing advice. Skills in contract and patent management may be required to protect the disseminated technology against subsequent diffusion, either inadvertent or deliberate, by customers and licensed suppliers.

The buyer, or user, of the transferred technology may need sophisticated technical expertise in order to absorb the knowledge provided by the supplier—that is, to embed the knowledge within its own organization—and subsequently to manage efficiently the equipment and functions in which it is embodied, particularly in areas such as the operation of complex machinery, shop layout, retraining of the workforce or recruitment of people with specific skills, use of appropriate materials in the right proportions, and quality control. The user may need skills similar to those of the disseminator in areas such as writing or evaluation of specifications and contract management. The originator may require users to develop adequate and costly safeguards against unauthorized rediffusion of the technology provided. Further, users failing to provide such required protection for confidential information may be vulnerable to costly legal liabilities.

Thus, successful dissemination of both embodied and embedded knowledge may be limited to innovators possessing certain communication and servicing facilities and to recipients with adequate absorptive capacity. Rubenstein [254, p. 395] notes that there appear to be substantial advantages to large size of firm on both sides of the transaction.

The motives for dissemination from innovators to users are those characterizing market transactions in general. Downstream users are customers—e.g., the manufacturers of diesel locomotives wish to sell them to railroads. Upstream users are suppliers—e.g., an airplane designer might construct the airframe itself, but subcontract for manufacture of the landing gear and electronic systems to its own specifications, divulging necessary information to the subcontractors as part of the process. Vertical dissemination is thus an alternative to vertical integration, just as are purchases of raw materials and sales of finished products.

Horizontal dissemination, or technology transfer in general, frequently takes the form of allowing another firm to produce a patented or otherwise proprietary product under license. If the innovator can prevent unauthorized dissemination of the licensed technology by its licensees or others, it loses none of the monopoly control of its knowledge by licensing, but merely chooses whether to reap the monopoly gains through profits on its own sales or through the royalty fees charged licensees. The innovator's choice will reflect any market or transmission imperfections favoring one means of exploiting the monopoly over the other, the degree to which mutual technological interdependence among the prospective licensor and licensees is recognized, economies or diseconomies of scale in direct exploitation of the technology and the relative sizes of the firms involved, and perhaps short-run differences in available productive capacity or operating costs.

Theoretical incentives for and effects of licensing have been explored in noncooperative duopoly game models. In an extension of Reinganum's 1983 model [244], Gallini and Winter [79] analyzed two primary incentives for licensing, the *ex post* incentive of replacement of inefficient production methods and the *ex ante* incentive of elimination of inefficient research expenditures. Since no firm is required to license, the *ex post* incentive can serve only to encourage additional R & D; but the *ex ante* incentive, or the prospect of being able to license the other firm's technology, may discourage R & D. In Gallini and Winter's model, licensing increases R & D when the two rivals' initial technologies are similar, but discourages it when their initial production costs are substantially different. The latter outcome may represent suppression of socially desirable R & D by high-cost firms. Katz and Shapiro's model [133] focused on the patent holder's decision to license its rival or refuse to do so, and on the effect of prospective licensing on the relative value of an innovation to the rivals and thus, in their model, which of the two obtains the innovation. In this model, minor innovations will be licensed between firms of similar efficiency; but major innovations—defined as those that would yield so great a cost advantage to the holder as to exclude its rival and result in monopoly—would not be, provided that the excluded firm is not so much more efficient than the owner of the innovation that it is more profitable to sell the monopoly than to exercise it. The rationale for this finding follows closely from that of Gilbert and Newbery [82, 83]. In Katz and Shapiro's model, the higher bidder always obtains the innovation. If one firm would exclude while the other would license, because of differences in efficiency, the result will always be exclusion, since a firm that would enjoy monopoly from the innovation will outbid the other.

Sellers in concentrated industries may use licensing and cross-licensing agreements to facilitate an oligopolistic consensus restraining price or nonprice competition in related products [236, 268, p. 453, 319]. Contrary to the outcome in Katz and Shapiro's non-cooperative game model, Wilson [336] found that major break-throughs entailing completely new products and processes, or radical improvements in them, are more likely to be licensed than are less drastic improvements. Further, royalty-free patent ex-changes are more likely, the fewer the rivals. Wilson interpreted the latter finding as suggesting cooperative oligopolistic behavior with limited non-price rivalry. Scherer listed "electric lights, glass bottles, parking meters, eyeglasses, magnesium, synthetic rubber, titanium paint pigments, radio broadcasting equipment, motion picture production, gypsum board, hardboard, machine tools, bathtubs, and a host of other electrical and chemical products" as among those "cartelized at one time or another" [268, p. 452] by such agreements.

The threat of imitation may prevent innovators from appropriat-ing the full monopoly value of technology transfer. Blackstone [19, pp. 98–112], Wilson [336], and Gallini [77] have all observed that licensing others to use a technology may be a means of preempting imitation. Such preemptive licensing could take the form of offering licenses to potential imitators at charges slightly less than the estimated costs of imitation, which may be well below the technology's monopoly value; or it could involve licensing others who might not otherwise enter the market, thus reducing the market share available to imitators. In a variant strategy, Xerox, which had successfully challenged RCA's claim to the basic patent on the electrofax duplicating process while also holding the patent on the superior xerography process, continued RCA's policy of liberally licensing manufacturers to produce electrofax machines but retained for itself exclusive manufacturing rights in xerography [20].

The market failure depicted in the model of pure disembodied knowledge as a tradable commodity [7] must be qualified in a world of embodied and embedded technology. The marginal, or transfer, cost is not zero; and thus welfare is not maximized by free dissemination. But the market failure identified is a real one. An extreme case is represented by complete suppression of a socially valuable innovation. Stories such as that of the unused and unlicensed patent for a razor blade that would last a year, reputedly held and suppressed by a major manufacturer of existing blades, or one covering a carbureter that would let a full-size car run 80 miles per gallon, held and suppressed by a major oil company, are the stuff of enduring economic legend. Real cases of suppression have been documented or convincingly alleged [29, 317, 319]; and models have been constructed in which suppression is rational monopolistic behavior, to prevent preemption of an incumbent monopolist's market by a challenger introducing a new product, for example [81, 82], or to force down the charge levied for a license to use a still better technology [13]. But in the great majority of the literature, the problem of suppression has been ignored, probably reflecting widespread agreement with Scherer *et al.*'s 1959 comment [277, p. 60] that "In the great majority of so-called suppression cases, however, critics have failed to recognize the presence of justifiable economic reasons for non-use," and Scherer's 1980 [268, p. 452] observation that "there are very few documented cases of the deliberate suppression of clearly superior innovations."

4.4. Imitation and the incentive to innovate

Unauthorized imitation is a major diffusion mechanism when patents are easily circumvented, when high litigation costs and uncertainties make patents little more than a "license to sue," and when "reverse engineering," or the analysis of how a competitor's product was made, is routinely pursued. Imitation may in some circumstances augment the net social benefits from innovation by speeding diffusion and expanding an innovation's ultimate spread toward the output level where the marginal social cost of adoption equals the marginal social benefit. But alternatively, by reducing anticipated earnings, imitation may retard the incentive to innovate.

The crucial roles of imitation, both beneficial and harmful, have long been recognized in the literature. The swarm of imitators is an essential part of Schumpeter's original vision of the economic development process [281]. Scherer, for example, described the idea that "the innovator performs [an] uniquely valuable social role by blazing the trail for risk-averse imitators" as "Schumpeter's most cherished thesis." [265, p. 3].

Brozen in 1951 [31] was perhaps the first to make the explicit distinction among invention, innovation, and "imitation" as the three essential stages in technology-based economic growth, and also to examine "imitation" systematically as a vital but relatively neglected step in the process. ("Imitation" is set in quotation marks, since modern usage substitutes "diffusion" for the concept as Brozen construed it.) Brozen's analysis of diffusion emphasized a well-recognized determinant of the rate at which new technology is introduced—the effect of sunk capital. As long as the equipment employed in an older process remains operable, a new process will not be introduced until its average *total* cost of production is lower than the older process's average *variable* cost of production. Thus, while older machinery is depreciating and being replaced, both the old and new technologies may be employed side by side. The more slowly an industry is growing, the slower will be the rate of imitation. In declining industries, imitation is slowest.

Reinganum [241, 242] has extended the analysis to investigate strategic reasons why even firms with identical capital characteristics might differ in dates of adopting new technologies. In determining the intra-industry diffusion rate, she postulates an industry of equal-size firms with identical equipment vintages and production costs. All face identical costs of adopting a new technology. In her model, the cost of adopting a cost-reducing process innovation falls over time, but the revenue stream to be obtained from adoption decreases with the number of rivals that have already adopted. Thus, each time a firm adopts the innovation, the remainder that have not yet done so find that their own optimal date of adoption has been pushed back. Since by assumption, they must adopt one at a time, the model determines a diffusion rate.

Fudenberg and Tirole [74] have modified Reinganum's model to allow simultaneous adoption or instantaneous imitation. In their duopoly model, each firm knows the date of adoption that yields the highest payoff, but considers introduction at a slightly earlier date to avoid preemption. If the gain from being the "leader," or the only one to have introduced, is high, successively earlier dates are considered, and one of the duopolists may introduce at the earliest moment when the net payoff to the leader is still positive. The follower introduces later, at a date that maximizes its profits, given that it must settle for having been preempted. Fudenberg and Tirole view this outcome as unlikely, given the possibility of coordination and the "credible threat of quick response" if one rival attempts to preempt the other. More likely, there will be a "joint adoption equilibrium" at the time when the sum of the payoffs to the two firms is maximized. In cases of more than two rivals, sequential diffusion is more likely than diffusion through simultaneous adoption. In a three-firm case, for example, a likely outcome is for one firm fearing preemption to lead, a second to imitate immediately, and the third to wait. But their model, like Reinganum's, is artificial and intended only to suggest possible reasons why there should be differences in adoption times among otherwise identical firms.

In yet another variant on Reinganum's model, Quirmbach [237] varied market structure on both the supplying and adopting sides of the diffusion process. In his model, as in Brozen's seminal work, a joint venture among adopters retards the rate of diffusion of a capital-embodied process innovation since it is in the cooperative interest of the adopters to protect investments in existing equipment. Since the joint venture does not take consumer surplus into account, the diffusion rate will be slower than socially optimal. However the rate at which a monopoly supplier will disseminate the innovation among competitive adopters is likely to be faster than the social optimum, since the supplier has no concern with protecting existing investments and adopters are concerned with preemption by others as well as the immediate advantages of the innovation. (As in Reinganum's model, both benefits and costs of adoption decline for later adopters—the latter more rapidly.)

Scherer's 1967 model [264], discussed in Section 2, was a pioneer contribution to formal theoretic modeling of firm R & D decisions under conditions including recognition that imitation is a strategic choice available to one or more rivals. The innovator's payoff function in this model included a known date of introduction for an imitator's identical product, the share of the market ultimately won by the imitator, and the rate at which the imitator penetrated the market. Among the outcomes for the duopoly case, assuming Cournot behavior, were 1) the shorter the imitation lag and the greater the imitator's expected market share, the greater was the innovator's incentive to accelerate its introduction date, provided it decided to engage in the project at all, and 2) the greater the would-be imitator's market share, the more vigorously it accelerated its imitation's introduction date when its existing sales were threatened by another's prospective innovation. "A dominant firm has little to gain by innovating," Scherer commented, "but much to lose when its position is attacked by a smaller innovator." [pp. 383–4].

Utilizing a slight reformulation and extension of Scherer's model, Baldwin and Childs [11] developed conditions under which imitation is more profitable than innovation. A short imitation lag, large market share, and rapid penetration rate relative to that of the innovator were all found to favor imitation. In their model, the larger the number of firms of roughly equal size, the less attractive imitation becomes relative to innovation. As the demand for existing products declines in response to the introduction of new ones, an imitative strategy becomes more profitable relative to innovation. Baldwin and Childs pointed out that while some of their results were intuitively obvious, the roles played in their model by the length of the imitation lag, the rate of market penetration, and relative rates at which sales of existing products declined all highlighted the value of a "fast second," or rapid imitation, strategy. Their analysis suggested that market structures under which the incentive to innovative would be entirely eliminated—i.e., in which all firms would opt for becoming fast seconds and none would do innovative R & D—are highly unlikely. More typically, at least one firm would recognize that if all adopted a fast second strategy and there was nothing to imitate, it could improve its profits by innovating, and it would do so even though it thereby raised by a still greater amount the profits of rivals who merely imitated. But, Baldwin and Childs continued, "the fast second strategy will serve to diminish innovative effort as the rivals try to wait each other out, bluff each other and shift strategies from time to time." [p. 23]. Baldwin and Childs made two highly artificial assumptions: that the costs of innovation and imitation were identical, and that a firm must choose between being an innovator or an imitator and cannot follow both strategies simultaneously.

In a 1978 article, Kamien and Schwartz [128, but see also 123 and 127] dropped the restrictive assumptions imposed by Baldwin and Childs, developing a richer and more detailed model of the innovation and imitation process. They let imitation be either more or less costly than innovation, and postulated that firms may engage simultaneously in both innovative and imitative R & D. They assumed further that innovations cut into existing product markets but do not necessarily eliminate them altogether, so that firms can choose whether or not to adopt the new technology and, if so, to what extent. Firms are allowed to revise their development programs and target completion dates, and thus their costs, if they are preempted by a rival. Solutions to these complex models were obtained through dynamic programming.

In the Kamien and Schwartz model, secure monopoly profits reduce innovative effort, protract development time, and discourage imitation as well as innovation. The difference between this last result and that of Baldwin and Childs, who concluded that market power encourages imitation, is not a contradiction, but stems from two structural differences. With Baldwin and Childs, a firm chooses between being an innovator and an imitator. If it chooses the latter strategy, it waits, without any expenditure on R & D, until a rival introduces an innovation. This strategy is not possible in the Kamien and Schwartz model. Rather, a firm embarks on an R & D project not knowing whether it will be a successful innovator, terminate the project on being preempted, or introduce an imitation after a prolonged lag or shortly after being preempted. (As in most R & D models, the shorter the time schedule for completion of either an innovation or an imitation, the greater the cost of the project.) The decision to imitate is thus conditional on preemption and the subsequent probability of successful imitation. Kamien and Schwartz show that, under their assumptions, the greater the firm's monopoly power in a market in which it continues to make sales, even though diminished by the innovation's penetration, the less the loss from rival preemption. Further, the stronger the existing position, the less the net gain in profit expected from introducing its own new product, now an imitation. Thus, the greater its market power, *ceteris paribus,* the more likely a firm is to abandon or postpone completion of a preempted project rather than accelerate it.

The 1978 Kamien and Schwartz model yielded other results directly relevant to imitation. Perhaps the most surprising is that a firm may attempt to innovate, even though imitation is more profitable. This result also emerges because the firm's objective is not to choose between mutually exclusive alternatives, but rather to decide when to begin an R & D program that could stochastically lead to the firm's being the innovator or, alternatively, being able to imitate promptly and at little additional cost. Thus, innovative R & D that does not lead to first introduction may nevertheless be necessary to be a successful "fast second."

Nelson and Winter [217, 218, 219] approach imitation from a distinctly different viewpoint in their simulation models of a Schumpeterian evolutionary process. Whereas Scherer, Baldwin and Childs, and Kamien and Schwartz all sought to develop insights into the types of market structure conducive to innovation or imitation, Nelson and Winter take the firm's choice between the two as part of a predetermined search strategy in which spending on R & D depends upon firm size; and they examine the long-run "feedback" effect of imitation in this context on industry structure. In their simulation runs, Nelson and Winter vary the initial number of firms, the ease of making major innovations, the ease of imitating, and whether the firms with the largest market shares exercise "investment restraint" in taking into account the impact of their output expansion on overall market conditions. Earnings are assumed reinvested under an automatic rule—either all earnings or, in the investment restraint case, at a rate predetermined by market share. New entry and its effects are ignored.

Nelson and Winter contrast the case in which the underlying technology is "science based" with a "cumulative technology" case. In the former, firms pay to "draw" from a pool of exogenously advancing technological possibilities by making R & D expenditures. In the cumulative technology case, the gain in productivity made possible by a successful draw depends upon the firm's present technology, which in turn reflects its past R & D successes rather than outside science. They also contrast situations of slow and rapid "latent productivity growth," or the pace at which new R & D opportunities emerge from forces exogenous to the actions of the industry's firms. Internal diffusion is assumed to be instantaneous and costless.

In general, relatively prompt and low cost, or "easy," imitation leads to lower degrees of final market concentration in the Nelson–Winter simulation runs, since it makes for a closer productivity race and thus greater similarity in company growth rates. Where the latent productivity growth is slow, and imitation is easy, imitators tend to be more profitable than innovators, but the latter are not eliminated. Rather, the market structure remains relatively stable if the largest firms exercise investment restraint. However, when the technical possibilities are rich, latent productivity growth is rapid, investment restraint is exhibited, the initial number of firms is large, and imitation is difficult, the gap in average productivity between the firms that perform both innovative and imitative R & D and those that are only imitators becomes large. As a result, the initial condition assumed, in which half of the firms are in each class, is unsustainable. Innovators who also imitate become more profitable and thus grow more rapidly, while those that perform only imitative R & D are gradually driven from the market.

When the largest firms in the Nelson–Winter model compete aggressively rather than practicing oligopolistic investment restraint, imitators end up with a substantially increased market share. This happens because, although an imitator can never have higher productivity than the most successful innovator, it does enjoy higher profits and hence more rapid growth than any innovator whose productivity it matches, since its R & D costs are by assumption lower. With innovators suffering low profits and a loss of market share, the amount of innovative R & D declines.

The effect of imitation also depends upon the nature of the "draw" from the technology pool. If technological advances are major and infrequent, which is modeled by making both innovation and imitation draws rare while technological knowledge continues to accumulate, each innovation has a pronounced impact on market structure and imitation is slow. Concentration increases, since a firm with a successful draw grows rapidly relative to the others for some time, and diffusion is slow. But under conditions of a "steady, gentle rain of technological advances" [218, p. 325], with numerous successful draws and only minor productivity gains associated with each, all firms—innovators and imitators alike—tend to grow at roughly equal rates. Nelson and Winter pointed out that such a phenomenon might lie behind what they referred to as the "Phillips hypothesis," or the finding discussed below that exogenous technological advances leading to sporadic major innovations fostered concentration in the aircraft industry.

Where initial producer concentration and R & D spending are high and imitation is easy in the Nelson–Winter simulations, an industry's average productivity level is close to the best-practice level, since by assumption 1) any firm that succeeds in either innovating or imitating the best practice available has a large market share, and 2) intrafirm diffusion is instantaneous. Similarly, in simulations with exogenous technological advances, the final average productivity level comes closest to best practice when imitators are more successful than innovators. This occurs because past innovative success has no effect on the payoffs from successful draws, while the effect of imitation on the diffusion of new technology is the same in both the science-based and cumulative technology cases. An occasional "hit" by an innovator, followed by widespread and aggressive imitation, will keep average practice in the science-based industry near the best available. This is a particularly interesting and intuitively appealing result, suggesting that the competitive effects of imitation might be most welcome in those industries where basic technological advances are induced by external developments. There are similar implications for industries in which most of the relevant R & D is financed by the government.

No one has yet combined in a single model the simultaneous short-run effects of concentration on imitation (which tend to be positive in the models of Scherer, Baldwin and Childs, and Kamien and Schwartz) and the long-run effects of imitation on concentration (which are generally negative in the evolutionary models of Nelson and Winter). Futia [75] made a promising start, although under far more restrictive assumptions than those of Nelson and Winter. He treated the probability that an innovation will be made as a function of the number of identical firms in an industry. In his short-run equilibrium analysis, only one firm wins the race to complete an R & D project; and successful innovation causes at least some, and possibly all, of the other firms to withdraw from the industry. Imitation is a longer-run phenomenon, engaged in either by new entrants or through the reentry of unsuccessful innovators. Entry by Futia's imitators lowers concentration in the very long run. He obtained an inverted "U" relationship between the ease of imitative entry (negatively correlated with long-run concentration) and the probability of innovation. This occurs because ease of imitation dampens innovation probabilities, and hence each firm's current R & D, while an increase in the number of firms raises the level of the industry's R & D activity.

4.5. Empirical studies of diffusion and industry structure

Beyond doubt, the most extensive empirical studies of the relationship between market structure and diffusion are the works by Mansfield and his associates. Among the major findings are the following.

A study of the diffusion of 14 major innovations in 4 industries [171, 174, 175, 178] indicated that the larger firms tended to adopt new innovations more promptly than the smaller ones, but not so promptly relative to their market shares as to accelerate the industrywide rate of initial adoption. (This phenomenon is further discussed by Davies [51, 52], with a numerical illustration replicated on p. 131. But the expected profitability from adoption, the growth rate of the firm, the current profitability of the firm and its profit trend, the average age of management, and the firm's liquidity, all hypothesized to influence the speed of adoption, turned out not to be significant explanatory variables.

The intrafirm diffusion of diesel locomotive usage among 30 railroads was shown to depend upon the expected profits of dieselization, the date of first adoption, firm liquidity, the age distribution of a firm's existing steam engines, and firm size [178]. *Ceteris paribus,* smaller railroad companies replaced their steam locomotives with diesels more rapidly than the larger ones. The negative partial correlation between firm size and the rate of internal diffusion may reflect the adverse effects of centralized decision making and diseconomies of managerial coordination, since the age distribution of steam engines would control for any tendency of the larger firms to have greater costs sunk in relatively young outmoded capital equipment (recall Brozen [31], Bain [8, p. 227], Fellner [65], and Salter [258]).

Romeo's study of the diffusion of numerically controlled (NC) machine tools in a number of using industries, described in Mansfield *et al.* [185], found that large firms tended to be early adopters, but slow internal diffusers, while late adopters, regardless of size, tended to "catch up" or complete intrafirm diffusion more promptly. The "industry" rate of diffusion, defined as the rate at which new NC machine tools replaced old ones throughout the industry, was positively and significantly related to the number of firms, but negatively and significantly related to differences in firms' sizes, both of which were interpreted as supporting the hypothesis that competition stimulates diffusion. Romeo [251] subsequently reported that a more "traditional" measure of diffusion, the rate at which first use spread among firms in an industry, was similarly related positively to number of firms and negatively to size differences, reinforcing the hypothesis that competition was conducive to rapid diffusion.

It has long been held that diffusion follows an "S" shaped, or sigmoid, curve over time, with the number of firms having adopted an innovation initially rising at an increasing rate, reaching a peak rate, and then rising at a decreasing rate approaching saturation. In an early study, Mansfield [171] reported statistical confirmation in a model that generated a symmetrical logistic diffusion curve and that treated diffusion over any given period as a function of the percentage of firms that had already adopted the new technology, the profitability of adoption, and the cost of adoption.

Mansfield's work indicates that relatively large R & D performers tend also to be prompt in imitating others' technologies. Imitation appears to be costly and time-consuming. In R & D projects Mansfield and his associates studied, the ratio of imitation to innovation costs averaged around 65 percent, while imitators' project development time was approximately 70 percent of the innovator's time. [188, 189]. The range is wide: in approximately half the cases studied, the cost ratio was less than 40 percent or over 90 percent. In one-seventh of the cases, imitation costs were greater than or equal to those incurred by the innovator, apparently because the innovator possessed substantial technological superiority. Patents held by innovators appeared to raise the costs of imitation, but not reduce its occurence appreciably. Mansfield and his colleagues found little evidence that original R & D was dampened by the prospect of imitation. Rather, "innovators routinely introduce new products despite the fact that other firms can imitate these products at about two-thirds (often less) of the time and cost expended by the innovator." [189, p. 910]. Among the firms in their sample, there was a widespread belief that innovation would be profitable even though imitators appeared within a few years.

Differences in the ratio of imitation to innovation cost were found to be related significantly to the proportion of research in the total cost of the original innovation. The greater the ratio of the costs of applied research to the remaining costs of introducing the innovation (product specification, pilot plant or prototype, plant and equipment, and manufacturing or marketing start-up), the lower the relative costs of imitation. Much of the innovator's research, Mansfield *et al.* observed, need not be duplicated by an imitator, but the other costs of introduction are as high for an imitator as they would have been if it were the innovator.

Mansfield and his associates discovered a highly significant positive relationship between an industry's concentration level and the ratio of imitation to innovation costs [182, 188]. Following Nelson and Winter, they hypothesized that ease of imitation relative to innovation should lower concentration. They also found, in corroboration of another Nelson–Winter model outcome, that "Science-based industries that spend a great deal on research and development may tend to have higher rates of imitation, holding other factors constant, than industries that are based on technologies more remote from science and that do little R and D." [185, p. 112].

In a 1979 study, Davies [51, 52] examined the diffusion of 22 postwar process innovations among using industries in the U.K. All of the processes originated in industries other than the using ones, many coming from abroad. In only 4 of the 22 cases were the innovations supplied by a single firm, and in all 4 of these the monopolized innovations were relatively simple and inexpensive. Davies found that while a symmetrical logistic curve such as found by Mansfield in his early work [171] gave a good fit to diffusion paths for major and complex innovations, a lognormal time path, with an earlier point of inflection and a subsequent period of steadier adoption rates, gave a better fit for the diffusion of simpler and less costly innovations. Davies interpreted his result as primarily reflecting the significance for major innovations of a "bandwagon" effect, or the competitive influence of the number of firms that had already adopted in accelerating the early rates at which others subsequently adopted, and the unimportance of this effect in the diffusion of minor innovations.

Turning to the effects of structure on diffusion, Davies confirmed Mansfield's finding that larger firms tended to adopt an innovation more promptly than smaller ones, but not disproportionately so.

"More specifically," he explained, "the results . . . suggest that a firm of size *S* will typically adopt earlier than one of, say, size $\frac{1}{2}S$. However, when compared with two firms, each of size $\frac{1}{2}S$, the larger firm will be slower, on average, than at least one of those firms." [52, p. 163]. The effects of industry concentration were "complicated" [52, p. 141], since Davies rejected single-number indices of concentration as misleading, and instead measured concentration by two variables, the number of firms in the using industry and the variance in firm sizes. He found that the fewer the number of firms, the more rapid the rate of diffusion, supporting the hypothesis of a positive relationship between that aspect of concentration and diffusion. But the relationship between size variance and rate of diffusion was negative, suggesting that concentration viewed as size inequality had a retarding effect on diffusion, measured as the percentage of firms that have adopted. He warned, however, that his results did not suggest that a duopoly of equally sized firms would be optimal, since the number of using firms was 20 or over in all but one of the 22 industries analyzed.

The empirical findings of others are consistent with those of Mansfield and Davies regarding the relationship between size and diffusion. In a study of diffusion rates for six process innovations among Swedish using firms, Nabseth [203] found that firm size exerted a positive and significant influence in only two cases. In a volume including case studies of ten innovations in six European countries [204, p. 21], the editors reported that the studies yielded "no definite evidence" that large firms were "leaders in . . . the adoption of new techniques." In some of the cases, the larger users were among the first to adopt, but in others this was not so. Terleckyj [307] found a sigmoid time path for growth of an industry's productivity (which he treated as an indicator of the diffusion rate) following introduction of an innovation. In an examination of the diffusion of radioisotope technology among hospitals, Rapoport [238] found that diffusion was more rapid in urban areas where a number of hospitals competed for status and doctors. Benvignati [15] traced the adoption of 33 textile machinery innovations by U.S. textile mills. She found that the large firms did adopt the innovations more promptly than the smaller ones, but that the differences between large and small firms were not as great as those found in other industries by Mansfield and Romeo.

Benvignati also reported that "technical concentration," or the proclivity of firms that adopted one innovation early to be early adopters of others, appeared to be weak in textiles. Adams and Dirlam [2], Oster [227], and Sumrall [298] all concluded that large size tended to retard diffusion of the basic oxygen furnace among steel companies.

The picture emerging from studies of the relationship between concentration and diffusion is blurred. Levin, Levin, and Meisel [145] found, in contrast to the results of Mansfield, Romeo, and Rapoport, but in confirmation of Davies, that diffusion of optical scanners to identify and price grocery items had been more rapid in the more concentrated of the 50 largest U.S. local grocery markets. In his study of West German manufacturing enterprises, Oppenländer [225] found that although small and medium-size firms (with less than 5,000 employees) were more prompt to introduce innovations than were large ones, the performance of the large enterprises in diffusion was superior. Market power, Oppenländer concluded, made it easier for a firm to induce others to adopt its innovations. But the large firms Oppenländer studied held a preponderance of blocking and fencing patents, and tended to favor other large firms over small and medium ones in granting licenses under these patents.

Angelmar [4], taking note of the findings of Scherer [263], Globerman [86], and Shrieves [289] that concentration had very little impact, and perhaps even a negative one, on R & D effort in industries with high technological opportunity, hypothesized that the effect of concentration in such industries would vary with the cost and uncertainty of R & D and with the ease and speed of imitation. Where costs and technical risks were low and barriers to imitation high, market power might not be needed to protect R & D investments and could, as posited by Scherer, reduce such investment by lessening the importance of speed of introduction. For a sample of 160 business units in high-opportunity industries, Angelmar found that concentration had a substantial and statistically significant positive effect on company-financed R & D as a percent of current revenue when R & D cost and uncertainty were high and imitation was prompt and easy. In contrast, the effect was statistically significant and negative in industries with high barriers to imitation and in which R & D costs and uncertainty were both low.

Two features of Phillips' study of the long-run impact of technological change on the structure of the U.S. commercial aircraft industry [233] warrant particular attention. First, he found that the main source of scientific and technological knowledge on which the industry's firms drew was exogenous, growing out of government-funded R & D on military aircraft. Second, successful entry by newcomers exploited "quantum leaps" [p. 90] in technology rather than imitation and minor improvements. As noted by Nelson and Winter, the outcome—increasing concentration, the spread of best technology occurring through the growth of successful innovators rather than adoption by other firms, and innovators gaining market share at the expense of imitators—was similar to the results yielded by their Schumpeterian models when the knowledge pool was augmented by sporadic and large changes in latent productivity rather than a steady "gentle rain" of small improvements.

Gort and Konakayama [89] examined the diffusion of seven major product innovations among producers, noting that diffusion at this level had not been studied as extensively as has diffusion among users. Drawing on the Gort–Klepper [88] study of life-cycle diffusion discussed below, they identified four principal determinants of the net entry rate up to the point of maximum industry participation. First, there is the "demonstration effect," or proportion of potential producers already producing the new product, which is hypothesized to encourage new entrants. Second, there is the extent to which technological change takes the form of technology transferable among firms because it is either proprietary but external to the industry or nonproprietary. They considered major innovations more readily transferable, and thus measured relative transferability by both number of major adaptations made after the new product has been introduced and patent counts. Third, accumulated experience, or learning by doing, was expected to give early producers an advantage and thus retard net entry. This experience was measured by cumulated production. Fourth, following Penrose [230], they expected adjustment costs of early adopters to rise more than proportionately with growth of firm. Thus, the more rapidly the firms that have already adopted are growing, the greater is the relative advantage of entrants. When their model was applied to data from the histories of DDT, lasers, nylon, penicillin, streptomycin, styrene, and transistors, Gort and Konokayama found that all four hypothesized effects were highly significant and indeed "explain most of the phenomenon of diffusion in the production of an innovation." [p. 1119].

International diffusion was examined by Tilton [312], Globerman [86], Teece [188, 305, 306], Mansfield and colleagues [188], Antonelli [5], and Dunning [60], among others. Reviewing the literature on the role of multinational enterprises in disseminating technology, Caves concluded that "Limited aggregative evidence suggests that the presence of MNEs is associated with more rapid diffusion of technical knowledge, at least in industrial-country markets." [36, p. 225].

In a study of the early history of the semiconductor industry, Tilton found that diffusion within the United States was rapid and accomplished mainly by small new firms, although the major innovations were made by large established firms. In Europe and Japan, diffusion was also speedy, but carried out through large firms. Diffusion from the United States to Europe and Japan was accomplished through licenses from U.S. innovators. Tilton attributed this willingness to license primarily to the highly competitive structure of the U.S. industry. Semiconductor markets at the time were fragmented and segmented, Tilton observed, so that licensees were more likely to compete with one another than with a particular licensor. Further, during the period Tilton studied, technological advance was so rapid and diverse that firms failing to grant licenses simply lost royalties to others that did license similar technologies.

Globerman examined the extent to which foreign ownership increased or decreased the R & D intensity of Canadian subsidiary firms relative to domestically-owned firms in the same industry. He found that in industries with high technological opportunities, foreign ownership led to increased domestic R & D effort. In the low opportunity industries, there was weak evidence of the reverse relationship. Globerman explained his results by noting that accessibility to foreign technology could either increase or decrease a domestic subsidiary's own R & D effort. In the high opportunity industries, subsidiaries appeared to engage in R & D aimed at adopting parents' products and processes to Canadian markets and conditions.

Teece studied technology transfer through dissemination by

multinational firms, including transfer to wholly owned subsidiaries, joint ventures, independent private enterprises, and government enterprises abroad. The costs of these technology transfers were defined as those of "transmitting and absorbing all of the relevant unembodied knowledge," which in turn was described as information relating to "methods of organisation and operation, quality control, and various other manufacturing procedures." [306, p. 245]. Technology embodied in such physical items as blueprints, tooling, and equipment was not included. In Teece's sample of 26 projects these international transfer costs tended to be high, averaging 19 percent of total project cost, up to and including manufacturing start-up, but ranging widely from 2 percent to 59 percent. Lower transfer costs were associated with previous experience of the transferor in transferring the particular technology, age of the technology, and the number of firms already using a competitive technology. The cost of transfer varied inversely with the size of the transferee, but the relation was not statistically significant. In some cases, the fall in costs with the number of previous transfers was quite large. Teece pointed out that this type of learning curve could put early projects at a cost disadvantage relative to later ones that benefitted from a transferor's increased skill in making the transfer.

In a 1982 book [188], Mansfield and co-workers, including Teece, reported results from several studies of various types of international technology transfer. They described diverse transfer channels, including emigration of knowledgeable people, export of goods and services embodying advanced technologies, licensing, and direct investment by multinational firms. The last has been the most rapidly growing transfer vehicle, and is now the leading one. Direct investment in overseas subsidiaries is preferred over licensing if the foreign market is big enough, as firms fear loss of valuable proprietary knowledge to potential competitors through licensing. For the same reason, firms are more willing to export goods resulting from new process technologies than they are to license the technology abroad. Licensed technology may be leaked to imitators, and the problem may be particularly severe abroad, since it is more difficult to determine whether foreign firms are imitating processes than products.

Mansfield *et al.* sought to identify the factors associated with the length of time taken in various countries for local firms to imitate a new product. This imitation lag was found to be inversely related to the amount spent on R & D relevant to the product in the imitator's own country, and to be shorter for more recent innovations. This latter result suggests that imitation has been facilitated by improving communications, transportation, and techniques of investment evaluation. The level of producer concentration in the imitating country had mixed effects, increasing the lag in one industry studied, reducing it in another, and having no significant effect in a third. Mansfield *et al.* suggested that the explanation for this inconsistent pattern might be that greater competition leads to more rapid imitation provided an industry is not too "fragmented" [188, p. 33] for its firms to engage in effective imitation.

Officers in a majority of the U.S.-based multinational firms surveyed by Mansfield and colleagues believed that the transfer of technology to a foreign subsidiary had little or no effect on the rapidity with which other firms imitated. But a minority of about 25 percent thought that transfer to a subsidiary had led to leaks in the host country through reverse engineering and the mobility of personnel, hastening imitation by an average of $2\frac{1}{2}$ years. Officials of 70 large British firms said they gained some technological capabilities as a result of such leaks from U.S. subsidiaries located in Great Britain.

Mansfield *et al.* reported that elasticities of cost with respect to time were greater for technology transfers than for original innovations and usually exceeded unity. These elasticities increased with the size of the firm initiating the transfer, whether transferor or transferee—a finding interpreted as indicating diseconomies of scale, particularly inflexibility by larger organizations in adjusting time schedules.

Antonelli [5] examined the diffusion of international data telecommunication networks among and within 40 U.S. and European multinational firms. The most prompt adopters were large U.S. firms with internal communications expertise that faced worldwide competition, consistent with the hypotheses that size of firm, home country in the country of origin of the technology, internal technological capability, and intensity of competition all encourage early adoption. R & D intensity had a positive but statistically insignificant effect on time of initial adoption, suggesting that the more specific form of technical competence in communications was of greater advantage to adopters. Late adopters, and smaller firms with more centralized managements, however, were more prompt in internal diffusion. Those who adopted late, Antonelli observed, enjoyed a more serviceable technology than the early adopters and were thus able to make prompter use of the network throughout their organizations.

Taking a long view, Dunning [60] distinguished five historical phases in the international transfer of technology. From the end of the Second World War until around 1965, according to Dunning, the multinationals tended to centralize technological knowledge in the parent company, limiting their overseas subsidiaries to inferior or widely-known technologies. Multinationals even bought up foreign high-technology companies and transferred their know-how to the home parent. Since the mid 1960s, the beginning of Dunning's most recent phase, the development and dissemination of technology accelerated. Japan has emerged as a technically advanced industrial leader, and firms in various countries of Latin America and Asia have become better able to make effective use of either their own or acquired technologies. As a result, technology transfer is increasingly occurring through advice and assistance, including provision of turnkey plants, to indigenous firms, rather than transfer through foreign subsidiaries. The response of the established multinationals to this new form of dissemination, according to Dunning, has been to diversify foreign operations through innovation, vertical integration, and local mergers. Thus, in Dunning's view, the source of the multinationals' market power is no longer possession of superior knowledge, but skill in transferring it abroad. He foresaw "a gradual dissemination of an increasing proportion of the world's technological stock, with a fall in the discretionary power of any one institution to exert [*sic*] monopoly rents from its own part of that stock." [p. 350].

Some writers, Dunning observed, have suggested that there may be economies of integration, including technology transfer, in substituting internal transactions for less efficient market ones. On the other hand, he continued, the integrated and diversified multinational corporations, with home country offices making decisions as to the technology to be transferred to subsidiaries, may be less sensitive to the technologies appropriate to individual markets and countries than other firms transferring technology to independent indigenous recipients. Recent studies from a large number of developing countries, reviewed by Pack [228], support the former view, finding little difference in choice of plant and equipment between domestic and foreign firms producing identical products. Indeed, Pack observed, since information about alternative technologies is difficult and costly to acquire, and often available in developing countries primarily if not solely from sales representatives of the larger advanced country producers, multinationals may have an advantage in selecting locally appropriate technologies. Parent firms may be able to identify machinery obsolete in one country but appropriate to another and transfer it. Experience in one country may be relevant to design of plant and machinery for another. And multinationals may obtain information as to locally suitable technologies from their subsidiaries' managers.

4.6. Diffusion over product and industry life cycles

Diffusion is a crucial feature in models applying a life-cycle approach to the analysis of R & D. In a leading contribution, Mueller and Tilton [198] identified four stylized stages characterizing the development of an industry created by a major innovation. At the first stage, that of "innovation," in which the new product or process is invented, developed, and introduced to the market, its spread is limited and perhaps inadequate, in part because the innate conservatism and "not invented here" bias of other firms retard diffusion. In Mueller and Tilton's second stage, labelled the "imitation" stage, uncertainty about technical obstacles and market potential fade. New firms enter in a "rush" [p. 574] shortly after a newly introduced innovation proves successful. They often offer different or superior variants on the original product or process. Typically, in this second stage, the underlying science and technology are poorly understood, and their pragmatic application does not require large-scale institutionalized industrial research facilities. Thus, small firms may be as successful as the large in entry through imitation. In the third stage, that of "technological competition," developments tend to favor the large industrial laboratories. The scientific and technological base becomes firmer, R & D becomes more specialized and sophisticated, and technical advance more commonly entails improvements in specific aspects of the basic technology. Knowledge becomes embodied in production experience. Small-scale imitation becomes more difficult. At the fourth and final stage, "standardization," patents expire, technological advance slows, the relevant scientific and engineering knowledge appears in textbooks, and production becomes standardized. Technological barriers to entry and imitation fall, perhaps to be replaced by barriers to entry such as economies of scale in production and marketing.

Utterback [318] offered a schema as stylized as that of Mueller and Tilton, but different in distinguishing between product and process innovations. In Utterback's industry life cycle, a new line of business begins with a major product innovation. In this early period, technical virtuosity, product quality, and flexibility in adapting the new products to users' needs are usually the most important attributes of business success, and the advantage commonly lies with small-scale, adaptable firms. As the basic product penetrates the market, standardization and lower-cost production processes become more important. At this stage, process innovation replaces product innovation, and greater efficiency is achieved through larger-scale and more capital-intensive methods of production. The mechanisms of diffusion, Utterback noted, differ for product and process innovations. New products are first introduced into small market niches, where they usually face little or no competition. Both through dissemination and imitation, the successful product spreads to new uses, coming more and more into competition with existing products as it does so. Process diffusion, which predominates in the later stage, takes the initial form of disseminating necessary knowledge to suppliers. These suppliers, or their imitators, may subsequently make the same technology available to competitors of the original innovator.

In a model emphasizing entry-exit patterns and considering only product innovations, Gort and Klepper [88] treat diffusion as occurring over a five-period cycle. Their stage I begins with initial commercial introduction of a product and ends when the number of entrants begins to rise sharply. In this stage, diffusion depends upon ease of imitation, size of the market, the number of potential competitors, and the speed with which technological information is communicated. Stage II covers a period of rapid growth in the number of producers. Gort and Klepper present evidence suggesting that this stage occurs in virtually all new product markets. The crucial questions for them are why such entry takes place, rather than having the market remain under the original innovator's control, and why the growth in numbers inevitably ends. In stage III, the number of firms is roughly constant as exit balances entry. At stage IV, exit exceeds entry, and so the number of firms falls. Stage V begins when the rate of exit declines to roughly offset entry once more, and the market reaches a mature equilibrium with a smaller number of firms than at intermediate stages.

Central to the Gort–Klepper model, and to the answers to their two key questions, is a distinction between information as organization capital and as human capital. The former adheres to a particular firm, either through patent ownership or because it is embedded throughout numerous places and individuals in the organization. The latter can be transferred from one organization to another by a knowledgeable individual. This distinction implies two types of information. I_1 in their notation stems from a firm's production experience and contains two components, one that can be appropriated by individual employees and one that cannot be, and thus remains the firm's property. The non-appropriable portion accumulates over time and serves as a growing barrier to entry by imitators. I_2 is information coming from sources other than current producers, which unambiguously facilitates entry. According to Gort and Klepper I_2 has been associated historically with major innovations, while I_1 typifies minor modifications. A life cycle is generated in the Gort–Klepper model by the growth of I_1 relative to I_2 over the product's life. Exit, becoming important in stage III, results from the decline in the number of external innovations, the growth of experience by existing firms, and a compression of profit rates. Thus, "the historical sequence, or time path, of events is viewed as a critical determinant of the ultimate structure of new product markets." [p. 630].

Formal life-cycle models that seek to identify general evolutionary principles applicable to a broad range of technological and structural conditions over extended time periods are of necessity highly abstract and stylized. Several empirical studies of life-cycle phenomena in the diffusion of technology have drawn on the insights of these models and tested their applicability.

Cortes [46] and Teubal [309] found evidence inconsistent with the view of Utterback [318] and Vernon [321] that standardization of technology and product characteristics increase in the mature stage of a product's life cycle. Cortes reported that there was no obvious relationship between product maturity and standardization of process technology in technology transfers to several Latin American countries. Both Cortes and Teubal found that product variety often increases with the maturity of an industry. Mansfield [182, 188] found that Vernon's [321] product life-cycle concept of international diffusion, in which export precedes offshore production, is becoming less common: more recently, new techniques are often first exploited outside the home country by foreign subsidiaries. In a 1979 article, Vernon [322] acknowledged that although his 1966 model had been appropriate for the era between the end of the Second World War and the 1960s, its rationale was not applicable to the succeeding age of rapid communication, growing worldwide technological sophistication, and pervasive multinational activity.

Rogers [250] applied the Mueller–Tilton model to a study of the exchange of technical information among California's "Silicon Valley" semiconductor firms. By the time of his study (the early 1980s), Rogers concluded, the industry had gone through the innovation and imitation stages, and had reached the third stage of technological competition. Standardization, the fourth stage, appeared to be setting in. The industry's evolution, as depicted by Rogers, followed the model quite well. "Innovation," he noted "was the main entry ticket to the semiconductor industry in the Silicon Valley in the 1960s and early 1970s, but this means of entry has become rare since the mid-1970s." [p. 112]. When the innovation stage was replaced by one of imitation, information needed by imitators was provided largely through the movement of personnel from firm to firm and through informal discussions, often over lunch or drinks, among the industry's scientists and engineers. The number of firms fell and average size rose with the development of technological competition, which Rogers, like Utterback, described as a stage in which process innovations developed in R & D laboratories became more important. This trend was acceleıated by the initial onset of standardization. From 1957, when Fairchild Semiconductor first located in the Valley, until 1973, the number of firms increased to approximately 70. After 1973, there was only one significant entrant. A process of merger and exit had set in by 1975, leaving only 10 independent firms producing semiconductors in the Valley by the end of 1979.

Benvignati [16] compared the U.S. diffusion rates of 22 major textile machinery innovations, finding that those of domestic origin diffused more rapidly than those originated abroad. Thus, she concluded, there may be a justification for policies promoting domestic R & D capabilities. Her observations, and the policy implications drawn therefrom, complement Mansfield's finding that the time taken for a country to imitate a new product is inversely related to that country's spending on R & D relevant to the product. Benvignati also found that the rate of diffusion was positively associated with using industries' sales levels, which, she hypothesized, was an indicator of capacity to use the innovation, but negatively with their growth rate. The latter result was consistent with Mansfield's hypothesis that an industry with too rapid a growth rate has no organizational slack among its firms to accommodate the experimentation needed to absorb a new innovation.

Gort and Klepper applied their five-stage model to the histories of 46 products. By comparing firm entry and exit rates with output growth, they tested the significance of economies of scale over the products' life cycles. They found that the Mueller–Tilton model, hypothesizing major, technology-induced changes in economies of scale, fit their observations far better than models assuming unchanging economies of scale or an optimal firm growth rate. However, increasing economies of scale did not seem to be a significant cause of the more rapid exit rate relative to entry at stages III and IV, since smaller firms were not a disproportionately large fraction of those exiting. Rather, Gort and Klepper concluded, the evidence supported their hypothesis that information embedded in firms grows relative to that possessed by individuals, raising barriers in the later stages to both entry and successful imitation by existing firms.

4.7. Summary and assessment

Diffusion is an essential step in technological change, and one that is difficult to deal with in assessing the link between business conduct and economic performance. The primary difficulty is the market failure analyzed by Arrow [7] stemming from the difference between optimal use of existing innovations and the limitations on imitation best suited to induce future innovations. This market failure complicates efforts to identify the diffusion process most conducive to overall economic welfare. Two basic elements of this process are in large part determined by structural characteristics of the originating and using industries, and are thus of primary concern here: the rate of diffusion, and the extent to which it occurs through dissemination or imitation. Absent a clear and generally accepted normative standard, analysts have been unable to specify optimal rates of diffusion or combinations of dissemination and imitation.

The import of the underlying theoretical problem for actual economic performance is lessened by the dubious relevance of one key assumption and one result of the model. First, the diffusion of technology does not involve pure disembodied knowledge with zero marginal cost of transmission. Rather, knowledge is embodied in products and processes that require learning to use efficiently, and it is embedded in records and memories that may be difficult to communicate accurately and completely. Diffusion is therefore both costly and risky. Second, despite the conclusion that the prospect of imitation dampens the incentive to innovate, Mansfield [188, 189] has found that in practice the prospect of imitation by rivals may be little or no deterrent to innovation.

Although their normative significance is unclear, the studies reviewed here reveal some basic relationships between structure and diffusion. Theoretical and empirical work suggest that technology diffuses faster, both by dissemination and imitation, in less concentrated markets. Competition may act as a double spur, since the prospect of imitation by rivals is a stimulus to preemptive dissemination. Yet competition also widens the wedge between the private and social values of an innovation, and this difference may lessen incentives for both innovation and diffusion.

In theoretical analyses, empirical studies, and the simulations of Nelson and Winter, high market share, small numbers of firms, and large firm size all make imitation more attractive relative to original innovation, whatever their effects may be on the absolute levels of those activities. But despite advantages that size and market power confer on existing imitators vis-à-vis innovators, the Nelson–Winter simulations suggest that in the long run, aggressive imitation generates a more competitive industry structure than does competition solely among innovators. The overall relationship between structure and imitation is thus a complex one, including an important feedback effect.

A number of distinctions in the literature have contributed greatly to understanding diffusion. They also provide valuable insights for future work. The following three seem most significant.

The traditional distinction between "product" and "process" innovation is often not as useful as that among "originators," "producers," and "users" of an innovation. The same technical advance may be viewed as a product innovation by its producers and as a process innovation by those using it. Originating firms may be located at either the producing or using level. Thus, diffusion may occur upstream to producers, downstream to users, and horizontally to competitors of the innovator.

The long-run effects of diffusion in industries with exogenous or science-based technology appear to be markedly different from the effects where the technology is endogenous or cumulative. Both Phillips' [233] empirical study and the Nelson–Winter [217, 218, 219] simulation models indicate the value of systematically identifying the sources of basic knowledge providing R & D opportunities facing industries, and of taking account of how differences in the "technology pool" affect diffusion and subsequently feed back upon structure.

Finally, the distinction between "organization capital," as technological knowledge embedded in a firm, and "human capital," as that possessed by individuals, has importance beyond its use in the Gort–Klepper [88] life-cycle model. It suggests, for example, that diffusion might take place in very different ways in the aircraft industry, where the technology is predominantly organizational (see Phillips [233], pp. 40–43), and in the semiconductor industry, in which human capital predominates and diffusion has been largely through movement of personnel among firms and informal contacts among their employees. Generalizations based on individual firm or industry case studies, therefore, may be misleading.

5. CONCLUSION

Technological progress counts, and as Schumpeter stressed, perfect competition therefore has no intrinsic claim to superiority. That vision is surely not debatable. But Schumpeter's notion that large, monopolistic enterprises would be the best engine of technological progress has led to much research, both theoretical and empirical. We summarize our views of this research, taken as a whole, here.

Absent detailed information unlikely to be known without great cost, or varying considerably across cases, one cannot say *a priori* whether more or less competition in R & D will improve economic welfare. Indeed, we cannot say whether more or less R & D would be better.

There is no unambiguous evidence of an important, generally valid, relationship between competition and innovative activity. Case studies provide thought-provoking possibilities. But where statistically significant relationships have been found, the explanatory power is small.

We do know that there are large and statistically significant differences across firms and industries in R & D/sales ratios. These differences may be the result of causal forces consistent with our theoretical models of market structure and innovation. The theories imply that the number and size distribution of sellers, barriers to entry, absolute firm size, and diversification lead to different innovative behavior and performance, given differences in environmental features such as the nature of the R & D process and the richness of technological opportunities. Since it is both difficult to measure competition and to control in statistical analyses for such environmental differences, it is possible that market structure is an important determinant of R & D investment, even though explanatory variables such as the number and size distribution of sellers, with or without control for other variables, do not have much statistical explanatory power.

It may be a mistake, furthermore, to accept the agnostic view that one cannot tell whether more or less competition is good without taking full account of specific circumstances. Theorists have examined special cases. A solution to the general model might show that, given some intuitively appealing and general definition of dynamic competition, more or less of it is unambiguously good. For when we know that the setting for variable *A* can have good or bad effects depending on the setting for *B*, we have not precluded the possibility that variable *C* (held constant in the analysis of *A* and *B*) would in the complete system always vary with *B* and *A* so as to impart a constant good or bad effect of *A*, regardless of *B*.

Prior research has examined only parts of the whole process of Schumpeterian competition. Greater understanding may come from thinking about the dynamic competition process. Schumpeter's vision was that the "process of Creative Destruction is the essential fact about capitalism." [283, p. 83]. Capitalism for Schumpeter [283, pp. 82–84] was "an evolutionary process," with "economic change" resulting "from the new consumers' goods, the new methods of production or transportation, the new markets, the new forms of industrial organization that capitalist enterprise creates." The process "incessantly revolutionizes the economic structure *from within,* incessantly destroying the old one, incessantly creating a new one." Economists, Schumpeter said, cannot examine the behavior of an oligopolistic industry "as if there were no past or future to it and think that they have understood what there is to understand if they interpret the behavior of those firms by means of the principle of maximizing profits."

Current R & D behavior reflects a past and a future as well as the present. Innovative investment must be understood in an evolutionary framework. Profit maximization may underlie R & D behavior, but Winter's work [337] suggests that some essential aspects of predicted market outcomes would remain valid even if innovative investment were regulated by "blind" rules of thumb.[21] The profit motive for innovation implies that innovating behavior (including subsequent diffusion) depends on economic opportunity (which is shaped by technological and marketing opportunities). An overall understanding of how market structure and technological change are related must come from understanding the mutual determination over time of market structure and economic opportunity.

We emphasize that studies to date, theoretical and empirical, have focused on parts of the complete picture. The failure of existing research to build holistic models severely restricts the usefulness of its results. The various pieces of the puzzle need to be put together. One might not be able to say anything about the effect of current market structure on performance, for example, if one did not include expectations about future structure. Many pieces of the R & D puzzle cannot be understood in isolation from the other pieces. High on the agenda for future research is the need for holistic models of market structure and technological change.

---

[21] Iwai [111, 112] provides further development of the evolutionary model.

References

References marked with a single asterisk denote works considered by the authors to be essential to an understanding of the field. Those marked with a double asterisk are also mentioned in the text but are not so basic to the field. Those references not asterisked have not been mentioned in the text.

[1] Adams, W. J., "Firm Size and Research Activity," *Quarterly Journal of Economics,* **84 (1970), 386–409.

[2] Adams, W. and J. B. Dirlam, "Big Steel, Invention, and Innovation," *Quarterly Journal of Economics,* **80 (1966), 167–189.

[3] Allen, Bruce T., "Concentration and Economic Progress: Note," *American Economic Review,* **59** (1969), 600–604.

[4] Angelmar, R., "Market Structure and Research Intensity in High-Technological-Opportunity Industries," *Journal of Industrial Economics,* **34 (1985), 69–79.

[5] Antonelli, C., "The Diffusion of an Organizational Innovation: International Data Telecommunications and Multinational Industrial Firms," *International Journal of Industrial Organization,* **3 (1985), 109–118.

[6] Armour, H. O. and D. J. Teece, "Vertical Integration and Technological Innovation," *Review of Economics and Statistics,* **62** (1980), 470–474.

*[7] Arrow, K. J., "Economic Welfare and the Allocation of Resources for Invention," in Universities-National Bureau Committee for Economic Research, *The Rate and Direction of Inventive Activity.* Princeton: Princeton University Press, 1962.

**[8] Bain, J. S., *Pricing Distribution and Employment: Economics of an Enterprise System,* rev. ed. New York: Holt, 1953.

[9] Baker, M. J., ed., *Industrial Innovation: Technology, Policy, Diffusion.* London: Macmillan, 1979.

[10] Baldwin, W. L., "Contracted Research and the Case for Big Business," *Journal of Political Economy,* **70 (1962), 294–298.

[11] Baldwin, W. L. and G. L. Childs, "The Fast Second and Rivalry in Research and Development," *Southern Economic Journal,* **36 (1969), 18–24.

*[12] Barzel, Y., "Optimal Timing of Innovations," *Review of Economics and Statistics,* **50** (1968), 348–355.

[13] Beck, R. L., "Patents, Property Rights, and Social Welfare: Search for a Restricted Optimum," *Southern Economic Journal,* **43 (1976) 1045–1055.

[14] Benoit, J. P., "Innovation and Imitation in a Duopoly," *Review of Economic Studies,* **52** (1985), 99–106.

[15] Benvignati, A. M., "Interfirm Adoption of Capital-Goods Innovations," *Review of Economics and Statistics,* **64 (1982), 330–335.

[16] Benvignati, A. M., "The Relationship between the Origin and Diffusion of Industrial Innovation," *Economica,* **49 (1982), 313–24.

[17] Ben-Zion, U. and D. J. Fixler, "Market Structure and Product Innovation," *Southern Economic Journal,* **48 (1981), 437–448.

**[18] Berle, A. A., *The 20th Century Capitalist Revolution.* New York: Harcourt Brace, 1954.

**[19] Blackstone, E. A., *The Copying Machine Industry: A Case Study.* Ph.D. dissertation submitted to the University of Michigan, 1968.

[20] Blackstone, E. A., "Restrictive Practices in the Marketing of Electrofax Copying Machines and Supplies: The SCM Corporation Case," *Journal of Industrial Economics,* **23 (1975), 189–202.
**[21] Blair, J. M., *Economic Concentration: Structure, Behavior, and Public Policy.* New York: Harcourt Brace Jovanovich, 1972.
[22] Blaug, M., "A Survey of the Theory of Process-Innovations," *Economica,* **30** (1963), 13–32.
**[23] Boston Consulting Group, *Perspectives on Experience.* Boston: Boston Consulting Group, 1968.
**[24] Bound, J., C. Cummins, Z. Griliches, B. H. Hall and A. Jaffe, "Who Does R & D and Who Patents?", in *R & D, Patents, and Productivity,* ed. by Z. Griliches. Chicago: University of Chicago Press for the National Bureau of Economic Research, 1984.
[25] Bowman, W., "The Incentive to Invent in Competitive as Contrasted to Monopolistic Industries," *Journal of Law and Economics,* **20** (1977), 227–228.
[26] Branch, B., "Research and Development and Its Relation to Sales Growth," *Journal of Economics and Business,* **25 (1972–3), 107–111.
[27] Branch, B., "Research and Development Activity and Profitability: A Distributed Lag Analysis," *Journal of Political Economy,* **82 (1974), 999–1011.
[28] Brander, J. A. and B. J. Spencer, "Strategic Commitment with R & D: the Symmetric Case," *Bell Journal of Economics,* **14 (1983), 225–235.
**[29] Bright, A. A. Jr., *The Electric Lamp Industry.* New York: Macmillan, 1949.
**[30] Brock, G. W., *The U.S. Computer Industry.* Cambridge, Mass.: Ballinger, 1975.
[31] Brozen, Y., "Invention, Innovation, and Imitation," *American Economic Review,* **41 (1951), 239–257.
**[32] Carter, C. F. and B. R. Williams, *Industry and Technical Progress.* London: Oxford University Press, 1957.
[33] Cave, J. A. K., "A Further Comment on Preemptive Patenting and the Persistence of Monopoly," *American Economic Review,* **75 (1985), 256–258.
**[34] Caves, R. E., ed., *Britain's Economic Prospects.* Washington: Brookings, 1968.
[35] Caves, R. E., "International Corporations: The Industrial Economics of Foreign Investment," *Economica,* **38 (1971), 1–27.
**[36] Caves, R. E., *Multinational Enterprise and Economic Analysis.* Cambridge: Cambridge University Press, 1982.
[37] Caves, R. E., M. E. Porter and A. M. Spence, *Competition in the Open Economy: A Model Applied to Canada.* Cambridge, Mass.: Harvard University Press, 1980.
**[38] Caves, R. E. and M. Uekusa, *Industrial Organization in Japan.* Washington: Brookings, 1976.
**[39] Clemence, R. V. and F. S. Doody, *The Schumpeterian System.* Cambridge, Mass.: Addison-Wesley, 1951.
[40] Comanor, W. S., "Research and Competitive Product Differentiation in the Pharmaceutical Industry in the United States," *Economica,* **31 (1964), 372–384.
[41] Comanor, W. S., "Research and Technical Change in the Pharmaceutical Industry," *Review of Economics and Statistics,* **47 (1965), 182–190.

[42] Comanor, W. S., "Market Structure, Product Differentiation, and Industrial Research," *Quarterly Journal of Economics,* **81** (1967), 639–657.

[43] Comanor, W. S. and F. M. Scherer, "Patent Statistics as a Measure of Technical Change," *Journal of Political Economy,* **77** (1969), 392–398.

[44] Connolly, R. A. and M. Hirschey, "Testing the Competitive Rivalry in R & D Hypothesis," Working Paper Series, Center for Applied Research, University of North Carolina at Greensboro, August 1983.

[45] Conseil National de la Politique Scientifique (CNPS), *Recherche et Croissance Economique.* Brussels: CNPS, 1965.

[46] Cortes, M., "The Transfer of Petrochemical Technology to Less Developed Countries," in *The Transfer and Utilization of Technical Knowledge,* ed. by D. Sahal. Lexington, Mass.: D. C. Heath, 1982.

[47] Craswell, R., "Antitrust Policy Issues Raised by Some Business Strategy Models," in *Papers on Business Strategy and Antitrust,* by E. Morrison and R. Craswell. Washington: U.S. Federal Trade Commission, September 1980.

[48] Culbertson, J. D. and W. F. Mueller, "The Influence of Market Structure on Technological Performance in the Food-Manufacturing Industries," *Review of Industrial Organization,* **2** (1985), 40–54.

[49] Dasgupta, P. and J. Stiglitz, "Industrial Structure and the Nature of Innovative Activity," *Economic Journal,* **90** (1980), 266–293.

[50] Dasgupta, P. and J. Stiglitz, "Uncertainty, Industrial Structure, and the Speed of R & D," *Bell Journal of Economics,* **11** (1980), 1–28.

[51] Davies, S. W., "Inter-Firm Diffusion of Process Innovations," *European Economic Review,* **12** (1979), 299–317.

[52] Davies, S. W., *The Diffusion of Process Innovations.* Cambridge: Cambridge University Press, 1979.

[53] Davis, K., "Competition, Monopoly, and the Incentive to Invent—Comment," *Australian Economic Papers,* **14** (1975), 128–131.

[54] Davis, K., "Competition, Monopoly, and the Incentive to Invent—Rejoinder," *Australian Economic Papers,* **16** (1977), 157.

[55] De Bondt, R. R., "Innovative Activity and Barriers to Entry," *European Economic Review,* **10** (1977), 95–109.

[56] Debrock, L. M., "Market Structure, Innovation, and Optimal Patent Life," *Journal of Law and Economics,* **28** (1985), 223–244.

[57] Debrock, L. M. and R. T. Masson, "Sooner or Later?, Inventive Rivalry and Welfare," *International Journal of Industrial Organization,* **3** (1985), 421–438.

[58] Demsetz H., "Information Efficiency: Another Viewpoint," *Journal of Law and Economics,* **12** (1969), 1–22.

[59] Donnenfeld, S., "Market Uncertainty and the Monopolist Incentive to Innovate," *International Journal of Industrial Organization,* **1** (1983), 379–386.

[60] Dunning, J. H., "Market Power of the Firm and International Transfer of Technology: A Historical Excursion," *International Journal of Industrial Organization,* **1** (1983), 333–351.

[61] Elliott, J. W., "Funds Flow vs. Expectational Theories of Research and Development Expenditures in the Firm," *Southern Economic Journal,* **37** (1971), 409–422.

[62] Enos, J. L., "Invention and Innovation in the Petroleum Refining Industry," in Universities-National Bureau Committee for Economic Research, *The*

Rate and Direction of Inventive Activity. Princeton: Princeton University Press, 1962.

[63] Evenson, R. E. and Y. Kislev, "A Stochastic Model of Applied Research," *Journal of Political Economy,* **84 (1976), 265–281.

[64] Farber, S., "Buyer Market Structure and R & D Effort: A Simultaneous Equations Model," *Review of Economics and Statistics,* **62 (1981), 336–345.

[65] Fellner, W., "The Influence of Market Structure on Technological Progress," *Quarterly Journal of Economics,* **65 (1951), 556–577.

[66] Fethke, G. C. and J. J. Birch, "Rivalry and the Timing of Innovation," *Bell Journal of Economics,* **13** (1982), 272–279.

[67] Fisher, F. M. and P. Temin, "Returns to Scale in Research and Development: What Does the Schumpeterian Hypothesis Imply?", *Journal of Political Economy,* **81 (1973), 56–70.

[68] Fisher, F. M. and P. Temin, "The Schumpeterian Hypothesis: Reply," *Journal of Political Economy,* **87 (1979), 386–389.

[69] Fixler, D. J., "Uncertainty, Market Structure and the Incentive to Invent," *Economica,* **50 (1983), 407–423.

[70] Flaherty, M. T., "Industry Structure and Cost-Reducing Investment," *Econometrica,* **48 (1980), 1187–1209.

[71] Flaherty, M. T., "Field Research on the Link between Technological Innovation and Growth: Evidence from the International Semiconductor Industry," Working Paper 84–83, Graduate School of Business Administration, Harvard University (mimeographed, no date).

**[72] Freeman, C., *The Economics of Industrial Innovation,* 2d ed. Cambridge, Mass.: MIT Press, 1982.

[73] Fudenberg, D., R. Gilbert, J. Stiglitz and J. Tirole, "Preemption, Leapfrogging and Competition in Patent Races," *European Economic Review,* **22 (1983), 3–31.

[74] Fudenberg, D. and J. Tirole, "Preemption and Rent Equalization in the Adoption of New Technology," *Review of Economic Studies,* **52 (1985), 383–401.

*[75] Futia, C. A., "Schumpeterian Competition," *Quarterly Journal of Economics,* **94** (1980), 675–695.

**[76] Galbraith, J. K., *American Capitalism: The Concept of Countervailing Power.* Boston: Houghton Mifflin, 1952.

[77] Gallini, N. T., "Deterrence by Market Sharing: A Strategic Incentive for Licensing," *American Economic Review,* **74 (1984), 931–941.

[78] Gallini, N. T. and Y. Kotowitz, "Optimal R and D Processes and Competition," *Economica,* **52 (1985), 321–334.

[79] Gallini, N. T. and R. A. Winter, "Licensing in the Theory of Innovation," *Rand Journal of Economics,* **16 (1985), 237–252.

[80] Gannicott, K., "The Determinants of Industrial R & D in Australia," *Economic Record,* **60 (1984), 231–235.

**[81] Gilbert, R. J., "Patents, Sleeping Patents, and Entry Deterrence," in *Strategy, Predation, and Antitrust Analysis,* ed. by S. C. Salop. Washington: U.S. Federal Trade Commission, 1981.

[82] Gilbert, R. J. and D. M. G. Newbery, "Preemptive Patenting and the Persistence of Monopoly," *American Economic Review,* **72 (1982), 514–526.

[83] Gilbert, R. J. and D. M. G. Newbery, "Preemptive Patenting and the Persistence of Monopoly: Reply," *American Economic Review,* **74 (1984), 251–253.

**[84] Gilbert, R. J. and D. M. G. Newbery, "Uncertain Innovation and the

Persistence of Monopoly: Comment," *American Economic Review,* **74** (1984), 238–242.
[85] Glennan, T. K., Jr., "Issues in the Choice of Development Policies," in *Strategy for R & D: Studies in the Microeconomics of Development,* by T. Marschak, T. K. Glennan, Jr., and R. Summers. New York: Springer-Verlag for the Rand Corporation, 1967.
*[86] Globerman, S., "Market Structure and R & D in Canadian Manufacturing Industries," *Quarterly Review of Economics and Business,* **13** (1973), 59–67.
*[87] Glover, J. D., *The Attack on Big Business.* Boston: Harvard University Press, 1954.
*[88] Gort, M., and S. Klepper, "Time Paths in the Diffusion of Product Innovations," *Economic Journal,* **92** (1982), 630–653.
*[89] Gort, M. and A. Konakayama, "A Model of Diffusion in the Production of an Innovation," *American Economic Review,* **72** (1982), 1111–1120.
*[90] Grabowski, H. G., "The Determinants of Industrial Research and Development: A Study of the Chemical, Drug, and Petroleum Industries," *Journal of Political Economy,* **76** (1968), 292–306.
*[91] Grabowski, H. G. and N. D. Baxter, "Rivalry in Industrial Research and Development: An Empirical Study," *Journal of Industrial Economics,* **21** (1973), 228–233.
*[92] Grabowski, H. G. and D. C. Mueller, "Industrial Research and Development, Intangible Capital Stocks, and Firm Profit Rates," *Bell Journal of Economics,* **9** (1978), 328–343.
*[93] Grabowski, H. G. and J. M. Vernon, "Structural Effects of Regulation on Innovation in the Ethical Drug Industry," in *Essays on Industrial Organization in Honor of Joe S. Bain,* ed. by R. T. Masson and P. D. Qualls. Cambridge, Mass.: Ballinger, 1976.
*[94] Greer, D. F. and S. A. Rhoades, "Concentration and Productivity Changes in the Long and Short Run," *Southern Economic Journal,* **43** (1976) 1031–1044.
*[95] Griliches, Z., "Research Costs and Social Returns: Hybrid Corn and Related Innovations," *Journal of Political Economy,* **66** (1958), 419–431.
[96] Griliches, Z., ed., *R & D, Patents, and Productivity.* Chicago: University of Chicago Press for the National Bureau of Economic Research, 1984.
*[97] Griliches, Z. and F. Lichtenberg, "Interindustry Technology Flows and Productivity Growth: A Reexamination," *Review of Economics and Statistics,* **66** (1984), 324–329.
[98] Hamberg, D., "Invention in the Industrial Research Laboratory," *Journal of Political Economy,* **71** (1963), 95–115.
*[99] Hamberg, D., "Size of Firm, Oligopoly, and Research: The Evidence," *Canadian Journal of Economics and Political Science,* **30** (1964), 62–75.
[100] Hamberg, D., *Essays on the Economics of Research and Development.* New York: Random House, 1966.
[101] Harris, C. and J. Vickers, "Patent Races and the Persistence of Monopoly," *Journal of Industrial Economics,* **33** (1965), 461–481.
[102] Heertje, A., ed., *Schumpeter's Vision: Capitalism, Socialism and Democracy After 40 Years.* New York: Praeger, 1981.
[103] Helleiner, G. K., "The Role of Multinational Corporations in the Less Developed Countries' Trade in Technology," *World Development,* **3** (1975), 161–189.
[104] Hennipman, P., "Monopoly: Impediment or Stimulus to Economic Pro-

gress?", in *Monopoly and Competition and Their Regulation,* ed. by E. H. Chamberlin. London: Macmillan, 1954.

[105] Hill, C. T. and J. M. Utterback, eds., *Technological Innovation for a Dynamic Economy.* New York: Pergamon Press, 1979.

[106] Hirshleifer, J., "The Private and Social Value of Information and the Reward for Innovative Activity," *American Economic Review,* **61 (1971), 561–574.

[107] Horowitz, I., "Firm Size and Research Activity," *Southern Economic Journal,* **28 (1962), 298–301.

[108] Howe, J. D. and D. G. McFetridge, "The Determinants of R & D Expenditures," *Canadian Journal of Economics,* **9 (1976), 57–71.

[109] Hu, S. C., "On the Incentive to Invent: A Clarificatory Note," *Journal of Law and Economics,* **16 (1973), 169–177.

**[110] Imel, B., M. R. Behr and P. G. Helmberger, *Market Structure and Performance: The U.S. Food Processing Industries.* Lexington, Mass.: D. C. Heath, 1972.

[111] Iwai, K., "Schumpeterian Dynamics: An Evolutionary Model of Innovation and Imitation," *Journal of Economic Behavior and Organization,* **5 (1984), 159–190.

[112] Iwai, K., "Schumpeterian Dynamics, Part II: Technological Progress, Firm Growth and 'Economic Selection'," *Journal of Economic Behavior and Organization,* **5 (1984), 321–355.

**[113] Jacquemin, A. P. and H. W. de Jong, *European Industrial Organization.* New York: Wiley, 1977.

**[114] Jaffe, A. B., "The Effects of Market Demand, Technological Opportunity and Research Spillovers on R & D Intensity and Productivity Growth," manuscript, March 1984.

[115] Johanisson, B. and C. Lindström, "Firm Size and Inventive Activity," *Swedish Journal of Economics,* **73** (1971), 427–442.

*[116] Jewkes, J., D. Sawers and R. Stillerman, *The Sources of Invention.* London: Macmillan, 1958.

[117] Kamien, M. I. and N. L. Schwartz, "Optimal Induced Technical Change," *Econometrica,* **36** (1968), 1–17.

[118] Kamien, M. I. and N. L. Schwartz, "Induced Factor Augmenting Technical Progress from a Microeconomic Viewpoint," *Econometrica,* **37** (1969), 668–684.

[119] Kamien, M. I. and N. L. Schwartz, "Market Structure, Elasticity of Demand, and Incentive to Invent," *Journal of Law and Economics,* **13 (1970), 241–252.

[120] Kamien, M. I. and N. L. Schwartz, "Expenditure Patterns for Risky R and D Projects," *Journal of Applied Probability,* **8 (1971), 60–73.

[121] Kamien, M. I. and N. L. Schwartz, "Market Structure, Rival's Response, and the Firm's Rate of Product Improvement," *Journal of Industrial Economics,* **20** (1972), 159–172.

[122] Kamien, M. I. and N. L. Schwartz, "Some Economic Consequences of Anticipating Technical Advance," *Western Economic Journal,* **10** (1972), 123–138.

[123] Kamien, M. I. and N. L. Schwartz, "Timing of Innovations Under Rivalry," *Econometrica,* **40 (1972), 43–60.

[124] Kamien, M. I. and N. L. Schwartz, "Patent Life and R & D Rivalry," *American Economic Review,* **64 (1974), 183–187.

[125] Kamien, M. I. and N. L. Schwartz, "Risky R & D with Rivalry," *Annals of Economic and Social Measurement,* **3** (1974), 276–277.
[126] Kamien, M. I. and N. L. Schwartz, "Market Structure and Innovation: A Survey," *Journal of Economic Literature,* **13** (1975), 1–37.
[127] Kamien, M. I. and N. L. Schwartz, "On the Degree of Rivalry for Maximum Innovative Activity," *Quarterly Journal of Economics,* **90** (1976), 245–260.
[128] Kamien, M. I. and N. L. Schwartz, "Potential Rivalry, Monopoly Profits and the Pace of Inventive Activity," *Review of Economic Studies,* **45** (1978), 547–557.
[129] Kamien, M. I. and N. L. Schwartz, "Self-Financing of an R & D Project," *American Economic Review,* **68** (1978), 252–261.
[130] Kamien, M. I. and N. L. Schwartz, "A Generalized Hazard Rate," *Economics Letters,* **5** (1980), 245–249.
[131] Kamien, M. I. and N. L. Schwartz, *Market Structure and Innovation.* Cambridge: Cambridge University Press, 1982.
[132] Kaplinsky, R., "Firm Size and Technical Change in a Dynamic Context," *Journal of Industrial Economics,* **32** (1983), 39–59.
[133] Katz, M. L. and C. Shapiro, "On the Licensing of Innovations," *Rand Journal of Economics,* **16** (1985), 504–520.
[134] Kitch, E. W., "The Nature and Function of the Patent System," *Journal of Law and Economics,* **20** (1977), 265–290.
[135] Klein, B., *Dynamic Economics.* Cambridge, Mass.: Harvard University Press, 1977.
[136] Klette, T. and D. de Meza, "Is the Market Biased Against Risky R & D?" *Rand Journal of Economics,* **17** (Spring 1986), 133–139.
[137] Kohn, M. G. and J. T. Scott, "Scale Economies in Research and Development: The Schumpeterian Hypothesis," *Journal of Industrial Economics,* **30** (1982), 239–249.
[138] Kohn, M. G. and S. Shavell, "The Theory of Search," *Journal of Economic Theory,* **9** (1974), 93–123.
[139] Lancaster, K., "Socially Optimal Product Differentiation," *American Economic Review,* **65** (1975), 567–585.
[140] Lange, O., "A Note on Innovations," *Review of Economic Statistics,* **25** (1943), 23–24.
[141] Lee, T. K., "A Welfare Analysis of Monopolistic R & D," *Economics Letters,* **12** (1983), 361–367.
[142] Lee, T. K., "On the Reswitching and Convergence Properties of Research and Development Rivalry," *Management Science,* **30** (1984), 186–197.
[143] Lee, T. K. and L. L. Wilde, "Market Structure and Innovation: A Reformulation," *Quarterly Journal of Economics,* **94** (1980), 429–436.
[144] Leffler, K., "Industry Equilibrium in New Product Research and Development: A Simple Approach," *Economic Inquiry,* **19** (1981), 60–76.
[145] Levin, S. G., S. L. Levin and J. B. Meisel, "Intermarket Differences in the Early Diffusion of an Innovation," *Southern Economic Journal,* **51** (1985), 672–680.
[146] Levin, R. C., "Technical Change and Optimal Scale: Some Evidence and Implications," *Southern Economic Journal,* **44** (1977), 208–221.
[147] Levin, R. C., "Technical Change, Barriers to Entry, and Market Structure," *Economica,* **45** (1978), 347–361.
[148] Levin, R. C., W. M. Cohen and D. C. Mowery, "R & D Appropriability,

Opportunity, and Market Structure: New Evidence on Some Schumpeterian Hypotheses," *American Economic Review,* **75** (1985), 20–24.

**[149] Levin, R. C., A. K. Klevorick, R. R. Nelson and S. G. Winter, "Survey Research on R & D Appropriability and Technological Opportunity: Part 1," Working paper, Yale University, July 1984.

**[150] Levin, R. C. and P. C. Reiss, "Tests of a Schumpeterian Model of R & D and Market Structure," in *R & D, Patents, and Productivity,* ed. by Z. Griliches. Chicago: University of Chicago Press for the National Bureau of Economic Research, 1984.

**[151] Lilienthal, D., *Big Business: A New Era.* New York: Harper, 1953.

[152] Link, A. N., "Firm Size and Efficient Entrepreneurial Activity: A Reformulation of the Schumpeter Hypothesis," *Journal of Political Economy,* **88 (1980), 771–782.

**[153] Link, A. N., *Allocating R & D Resources: A Study of the Determinants of R & D by Character of Use.* Washington: U.S. National Science Foundation, 1981.

**[154] Link, A. N., *Research and Development in U.S. Manufacturing.* New York: Praeger, 1981.

[155] Link, A. N., "A Disaggregated Analysis of Industrial R & D: Product versus Process Innovation," in *The Transfer and Utilization of Technical Knowledge,* ed. by D. Sahal. Lexington, Mass.: D. C. Heath, 1982.

[156] Link, A. N., "An Analysis of the Composition of R & D Spending," *Southern Economic Journal,* **49 (1982), 342–348.

[157] Link, A. N., "Alternative Sources of Technology: An Analysis of Induced Innovations," *Managerial and Decision Economics,* **4 (1983), 40–43.

[158] Link, A. N. and J. E. Long, "The Simple Economics of Basic Scientific Research: A Test of Nelson's Diversification Hypothesis," *Journal of Industrial Economics,* **30 (1981), 105–109.

[159] Link, A. N. and J. Lunn, "Concentration and the Returns to R & D," *Review of Industrial Organization,* **1 (1984), 232–239.

[160] Loeb, P. D. and V. Lin, "Research and Development in the Pharmaceutical Industry—A Specification Error Approach," *Journal of Industrial Economics,* **26 (1977), 45–51.

**[161] Long, W. F., "The Effects of Inter-firm Cooperation and Economies of Scale on Product Improving Research and Development Expenditures," mimeographed, December 1981.

*[162] Loury, G. C., "Market Structure and Innovation," *Quarterly Journal of Economics,* **93** (1979), 395–410.

[163] Lunn, J., "Research and Development and the Schumpeterian Hypothesis: Alternate Approach," *Southern Economic Journal,* **49** (1982), 209–217.

[164] Lunn, J., "Market Structure and the Incentive to Invent," *Eastern Economic Journal,* **9 (1983), 333–336.

[165] Lunn, J., "An Empirical Analysis of Process and Product Patenting: A Simultaneous Equation Framework," *Journal of Industrial Economics,* **34 (1986), 319–330.

[166] Lunn, J. and S. Martin, "Market Structure, Firm Structure, and Research Development," *Quarterly Review of Economics and Business,* **26 (1986), 31–44.

[167] MacDonald, J. M., "R & D and the Directions of Diversification," *Review of Economics and Statistics,* **67 (1985), 583–590.

**[168] Machlup, F., *Knowledge: Its Creation, Distribution, and Economic*

Significance, vol. I, *Knowledge and Knowledge Production*. Princeton: Princeton University Press, 1980.

*[169] Maclaurin, W. R., *Invention and Innovation in the Radio Industry*, New York: Macmillan, 1949.

*[170] Maclaurin, W. R., "Technological Progress in Some American Industries," *American Economic Review*, **44** (1954), 178–189.

*[171] Mansfield, E., "Technical Change and the Rate of Imitation," *Econometrica*, **29** (1961), 741–766.

[172] Mansfield, E., "Entry, Gibrat's Law, Innovation, and the Growth of Firms," *American Economic Review*, **52** (1962), 1023–1051.

[173] Mansfield, E., "Intrafirm Rates of Diffusion of an Innovation," *Review of Economics and Statistics*, **45** (1963), 348–359.

*[174] Mansfield, E., "Size of Firm, Market Structure, and Innovation," *Journal of Political Economy*, **71** (1963), 556–576.

*[175] Mansfield, E., "The Speed of Response of Firms to New Techniques," *Quarterly Journal of Economics*, **77** (1963), 290–311.

[176] Mansfield, E., "Industrial Research and Development Expenditures: Determinants, Prospects, and Relation of Size of Firm and Inventive Output," *Journal of Political Economy*, **72** (1964), 319–340.

[177] Mansfield, E., *Econometric Studies of Industrial Research and Technological Innovation*. New York: Norton, 1967.

*[178] Mansfield, E., *Industrial Research and Technological Innovation: An Econometric Analysis*. New York: Norton, 1968.

*[179] Mansfield, E., *The Economics of Technical Change*. New York: Norton, 1968.

*[180] Mansfield, E., "Basic Research and Productivity Increase in Manufacturing," *American Economic Review*, **70** (1980), 863–873.

*[181] Mansfield, E., "Composition of R and D Expenditures: Relationship to Size of Firm, Concentration, and Innovative Output," *Review of Economics and Statistics*, **63** (1981), 610–615.

*[182] Mansfield, E., "Technology Transfer, Innovation, and Public Policy," in *The Transfer and Utilization of Technical Knowledge*, ed. by D. Sahal. Lexington, Mass.: D. C. Heath, 1982.

*[183] Mansfield, E., "Technological Change and Market Structure: An Empirical Study," *American Economic Review*, **73** (1983), 205–209.

[184] Mansfield, E., "R & D and Innovation: Some Empirical Findings," in *R & D, Patents, and Productivity*, ed. by Z. Griliches. Chicago: University of Chicago Press for the National Bureau of Economic Research, 1984.

*[185] Mansfield, E., J. Rapoport, A. Romeo, E. Villani, S. Wagner and F. Husic, *The Production and Application of New Industrial Technologies*. New York: Norton, 1977.

*[186] Mansfield, E., J. Rapoport, A. Romeo, S. Wagner and G. Beardsley, "Social and Private Rates of Return from Industrial Innovations," *Quarterly Journal of Economics*, **91** (1977), 221–240.

*[187] Mansfield, E., J. Rapoport, J. Schnee, S. Wagner and M. Hamburger, *Research and Innovation in the Modern Corporation*. New York: Norton, 1971.

*[188] Mansfield, E., A. Romeo, M. Schwartz, D. Teece, S. Wagner, and P. Brach, *Technology Transfer, Productivity, and Economic Policy*. New York: Norton, 1982.

[189] Mansfield, E., M. Schwartz and S. Wagner, "Imitation Costs and Patents: An Empirical Study," *Economic Journal,* **91 (1981), 907–918.
[190] Markham, J. W., "Market Structure, Business Conduct, and Innovation," *American Economic Review,* **55 (1965), 323–332.
[191] Mason, E. S., "Price and Production Policies of Large-Scale Enterprise," *American Economic Review,* **29 (1939), 61–74.
[192] Mason, E. S., "Schumpeter on Monopoly and the Large Firm," *Review of Economics and Statistics,* **33** (1951), 139–144.
[193] McEachern, W. A. and A. A. Romeo, "Stockholder Control, Uncertainty and the Allocation of Resources to Research and Development," *Journal of Industrial Economics,* **26 (1978) 349–361.
[194] Meisel, J. B. and S. A. Y. Lin, "The Impact of Market Structure on the Firm's Allocation of Resources to Research and Development," *Quarterly Review of Economics and Business,* **23** (1983), 28–43.
**[195] Mogee, M. E., "The Process of Technological Innovation in Industry: A State-of-Knowledge Review for Congress," in U.S. Congress, Joint Economic Committee, *Special Study on Economic Change,* 3, *Research and Innovation: Developing a Dynamic Nation.* Washington: U.S. Government Printing Office, 1980.
[196] Morand, J. C., "La Recherche et le Développement Selon la Dimension des Enterprises," *Le Progrès Scientifique,* **122** (1968).
[197] Mueller, D. C., "Patents, Research and Development, and the Measurement of Inventive Activity," *Journal of Industrial Economics,* **15 (1966), 26–37.
[198] Mueller, D. C. and J. E. Tilton, "Research and Development Costs as a Barrier to Entry," *Canadian Journal of Economics,* **2 (1969), 570–579.
[199] Mueller, W. F., "A Case Study of Product Discovery and Innovation Costs," *Southern Economic Journal,* **24 (1957), 80–86.
**[200] Mueller, W. F., "The Origins of the Basic Inventions Underlying Du Pont's Major Product and Process Innovations," in Universities-National Bureau Committee for Economic Research: *The Rate and Direction of Inventive Activity.* Princeton: Princeton University Press, 1962.
[201] Mueller, W. F., J. Culbertson and B. Peckham, *Market Structure and Technological Performance in the Food Manufacturing Industries.* North Central Regional Research Publication 280, University of Wisconsin-Madison, 1982.
[202] Mukhopadhyay, A. K., "Technological Progress and Change in Market Concentration in the U.S., 1963–77," *Southern Economic Journal,* **52 (1985), 141–149.
**[203] Nabseth, L., "The Diffusion of Innovations in Swedish Industry," in *Science and Technology in Economic Growth,* ed. by B. R. Williams. London: Macmillan, 1973.
**[204] Nabseth, L. and G. F. Ray, eds., *The Diffusion of New Industrial Processes: An International Study.* Cambridge: Cambridge University Press, 1974.
[205] Needham, D., "Market Structure and Firms' R & D Behavior," *Journal of Industrial Economics,* **23 (1975), 241–255.
[206] Nelson, R. R., "The Economics of Invention," *Journal of Business,* **32** (1959), 101–127.
[207] Nelson, R. R., "The Simple Economics of Basic Scientific Research," *Journal of Political Economy,* **67 (1959), 297–306.
**[208] Nelson, R. R., "Uncertainty, Learning, and the Economics of Parallel

Research and Development Efforts," *Review of Economics and Statistics,* **43** (1961), 351–364.

[209] Nelson, R. R., "The Allocation of Research and Development Resources: Some Problems of Public Policy," in *Economics of Research and Development,* ed. by R. A. Tybout. Columbus: Ohio State University Press, 1965.

[210] Nelson, R. R., "Issues and Suggestions for the Study of Industrial Organization in a Regime of Rapid Technical Change," in *Policy Issues and Research Opportunities in Industrial Organization,* ed. by V. Fuchs. New York: National Bureau of Economic Research, 1972.

[211] Nelson, R. R., "Research on Productivity Growth and Productivity Differences: Dead Ends and New Departures," *Journal of Economic Literature,* **19** (1981), 1029–1064.

[212] Nelson, R. R., ed., *Government and Technical Progress: A Cross-Industry Analysis.* New York: Pergamon, 1982.

[213] Nelson, R. R., "The Role of Knowledge in R & D Efficiency," *Quarterly Journal of Economics,* **97** (1982), 453–470.

[214] Nelson, R. R., M. J. Peck and E. D. Kalachek, *Technology, Economic Growth, and Public Policy.* Washington: Brookings, 1967.

[215] Nelson, R. R. and S. G. Winter, "Toward an Evolutionary Theory of Economic Capabilities," *American Economic Review,* **63** (1973), 440–449.

[216] Nelson, R. R. and S. G. Winter, "Growth Theory from an Evolutionary Perspective: the Differential Productivity Puzzle," *American Economic Review,* **65** (1975), 338–344.

[217] Nelson, R. R. and S. G. Winter, "Forces Generating and Limiting Concentration Under Schumpeterian Competition," *Bell Journal of Economics,* **9** (1978), 524–548.

[218] Nelson, R. R. and S. G. Winter, *An Evolutionary Theory of Economic Change.* Cambridge, Mass.: Harvard University Press, 1982.

[219] Nelson, R. R. and S. G. Winter, "The Schumpeterian Tradeoff Revisited," *American Economic Review,* **72** (1982), 114–132.

[220] Nelson, R. R., S. G. Winter and H. L. Schuette, "Technical Change in an Evolutionary Model," *Quarterly Journal of Economics,* **90** (1976), 90–118.

[221] Neumann, M., I. Böbel and A. Haid, "Innovations and Market Structure in West German Industries," *Managerial and Decision Economics,* **3** (1982), 131–139.

[222] Ng, Y. L., "Competition, Monopoly, and the Incentive to Invent," *Australian Economic Papers,* **10** (1971), 45–50.

[223] Ng, Y. L., "Competition, Monopoly, and the Incentive to Invent—Reply," *Australian Economic Papers,* **16** (1977), 154–156.

[224] Nutter, G. W., "Monopoly, Bigness, and Progress," *Journal of Political Economy,* **64** (1956), 520–527.

[225] Oppenländer, K. H., "Das Verhalten Kleiner und Mittlerer Unternehmen im Industriellenprozess." Paper presented at a conference, Die Gesamtwirtschaftliche Funktion Kleiner und Mittlerer Unternehmen, Ifo-Institut für Wirtschaftforschung, Munich, West Germany, October 8–10, 1975.

[226] Ordover, J. A. and R. D. Willig, "An Economic Definition of Predatory Product Innovation," in *Strategy, Predation, and Antitrust Analysis,* ed. by S. C. Salop. Washington: U.S. Federal Trade Commission, 1981.

[227] Oster, S., "The Diffusion of Innovation among Steel Firms: The Basic Oxygen Furnace," *Bell Journal of Economics,* **13** (1982), 45–56.

[228] Pack, H., "Appropriate Industrial Technology: Benefits and Obstacles," *Annals of the American Academy of Political and Social Science,* **458 (1981), 27–40.

**[229] Peck, M. J., "Inventions in the Postwar American Aluminum Industry," in Universities-National Bureau Committee for Economic Research, *The Rate and Direction of Inventive Activity*. Princeton: Princeton University Press, 1962.

**[230] Penrose, E. T., *The Theory of the Growth of the Firm*. Oxford: Blackwell, 1959.

[231] Phillips, A., "Concentration, Scale, and Technological Change in Selected Manufacturing Industries, 1899–1939," *Journal of Industrial Economics,* **5 (1956), 179–193.

[232] Phillips, A., "Patents, Potential Competition, and Technical Progress," *American Economic Review,* **56 (1966), 301–310.

*[233] Phillips, A., *Technology and Market Structure*. Lexington, Mass.: D. C. Heath, 1971.

[234] Phlips, L., "Concentration, Dimension, et Recherche dans l'Industrie Manufacturière Belge," *Recherches Economiques de Lourain,* **1** (1969).

**[235] Phlips, L., *Effects of Industrial Concentration: A Cross-section Analysis for the Common Market*. Amsterdam: North-Holland, 1971.

[236] Priest, G. L., "Cartels and Patent License Agreements," *Journal of Law and Economics,* **20 (1977), 309–378.

[237] Quirmbach, H. C., "The Diffusion of New Technology and the Market for an Innovation," *Rand Journal of Economics,* **17 (1986), 33–47.

[238] Rapoport, J., "Diffusion of Technological Innovation among Nonprofit Firms: A Case Study of Radioisotopes in U.S. Hospitals," *Journal of Economics and Business,* **30 (1978), 108–118.

[239] Ravenscraft, D. and F. M. Scherer, "The Lag Structure of Returns to Research and Development," *Applied Economics,* **14 (1982), 603–620.

[240] Reinganum, J. F., "Dynamic Games of Innovation," *Journal of Economic Theory,* **25 (1981), 21–41.

[241] Reinganum, J. F., "Market Structure and the Diffusion of New Technology," *Bell Journal of Economics,* **12 (1981), 618–624.

[242] Reinganum, J. F., "On the Diffusion of a New Technology: A Game Theoretic Approach," *Review of Economic Studies,* **48 (1981), 395–405.

[243] Reinganum, J. F., "A Dynamic Game of R & D: Patent Protection and Competitive Behavior," *Econometrica,* **50 (1982), 671–688.

[244] Reinganum, J. F., "Technology Adoption Under Imperfect Information," *Bell Journal of Economics,* **14 (1983), 57–69.

[245] Reinganum, J. F., "Uncertain Innovation and the Persistence of Monopoly," *American Economic Review,* **73 (1983), 741–748.

[246] Reinganum, J. F., "Uncertain Innovation and the Persistence of Monopoly: Reply," *American Economic Review,* **74 (1984), 243–246.

[247] Reinganum, J. F., "A Two-Stage Model of Research and Development with Endogenous Second-Mover Advantages," *International Journal of Industrial Organization,* **3 (1985), 275–292.

[248] Reinganum, J. F., "Innovation and Industry Evolution," *Quarterly Journal of Economics,* **100 (1985), 81–99.

[249] Rodriguez, C. A., "A Comment on Fisher and Temin on the Schumpeterian Hypothesis," *Journal of Political Economy,* **87 (1979), 383–385.

**[250] Rogers, E. M., "Information Exchange and Technological Innovation," in

The Transfer and Utilization of Technical Knowledge, ed. by D. Sahal. Lexington, Mass.: D. C. Heath, 1982.

[251] Romeo, A. A., "The Rate of Imitation of a Capital-Embodied Process Innovation," *Economica,* **44 (1977), 63–69.

[252] Rosenberg, J. B., "Research and Market Share: A Reappraisal of the Schumpeterian Hypothesis," *Journal of Industrial Economics,* **25** (1976), 101–112.

[253] Rosenberg, N., ed., *The Economics of Technical Change.* Harmondsworth, England: Penguin, 1971.

**[254] Rubenstein, A. H., "The Role of Embedded Technology in the Industrial Innovation Process," in U.S. Congress, Joint Economic Committee, *Special Study on Economic Change, 3, Research and Innovation: Developing a Dynamic Nation.* Washington: U.S. Government Printing Office, 1980.

[255] Ruttan, V. W., "Usher and Schumpeter on Invention, Innovation, and Technological Change," *Quarterly Journal of Economics,* **73** (1959), 596–606.

**[256] Sahal, D., ed., *The Transfer and Utilization of Technical Knowledge.* Lexington, Mass.: D. C. Heath, 1982.

[257] Salant, S. W., "Preemptive Patenting and the Persistence of Monopoly: Comment," *American Economic Review,* **74 (1984), 247–250.

**[258] Salter, W. E. G., *Productivity and Technical Change.* Cambridge: Cambridge University Press, 1960.

**[259] Sanders, B. S., "Some Difficulties in Measuring Innovative Activity," in Universities-National Bureau Committee for Economic Research, *The Rate and Direction of Innovative Activity.* Princeton: Princeton University Press, 1962.

[260] Sato, R. and S. Tsutsui, "Technical Progress, the Schumpeterian Hypothesis, and Market Structure," *Zeitschrift für Nationalökonomie,* **44** supp. (1984), 1–37.

*[261] Scherer, F. M., "Firm Size, Market Structure, Opportunity, and the Output of Patented Inventions," *American Economic Review,* **55** (1965), 1097–1125.

[262] Scherer, F. M., "Size of Firm, Oligopoly, and Research: A Comment," *Canadian Journal of Economics and Political Science,* **31** (1965), 256–266.

*[263] Scherer, F. M., "Market Structure and the Employment of Scientists and Engineers," *American Economic Review,* **57** (1967), 524–531.

*[264] Scherer, F. M., "Research and Development Resource Allocation Under Rivalry," *Quarterly Journal of Economics,* **81** (1967), 359–394.

**[265] Scherer, F. M., *Research and Development Returns to Scale and the Schumpeterian Hypothesis: Comment.* Berlin: International Institute of Management, 1973.

**[266] Scherer, F. M., *The Economic Effects of Compulsory Patent Licensing.* New York: New York University Graduate School of Business, 1977.

[267] Scherer, F. M., "The Welfare Economics of Product Variety: An Application to the Ready-to-Eat Cereals Industry," *Journal of Industrial Economics,* **28 (1979), 113–134.

**[268] Scherer, F. M., *Industrial Market Structure and Economic Performance,* 2d ed. Chicago: Rand McNally, 1980.

[269] Scherer, F. M., "Demand-Pull and Technological Innovation: Schmookler Revisited," *Journal of Industrial Economics,* **30** (1982), 225–237.

[270] Scherer, F. M., "Inter-Industry Technology Flows in the United States," *Research Policy,* **11 (1982), 227–245.

[271] Scherer, F. M., "Concentration, R & D, and Productivity Change," *Southern Economic Journal,* **50 (1983), 221–225.

[272] Scherer, F. M., "The Propensity to Patent," *International Journal of Industrial Organization,* **1 (1983), 107–128.

*[273] Scherer, F. M., *Innovation and Growth: Schumpeterian Perspectives.* Cambridge, Mass.: MIT Press, 1984.

**[274] Scherer, F. M., "Technological Change and the Modern Corporation," in *The Impact of the Modern Corporation,* ed. by B. Bock, H. J. Goldschmid, I. Millstein, and F. M. Scherer. New York: Columbia University Press, 1984.

[275] Scherer, F. M., "Using Linked Patent and R & D Data to Measure Interindustry Technology Flows," in *R & D, Patents, and Productivity,* ed. by Z. Griliches. Chicago: University of Chicago Press for the National Bureau of Economic Research, 1984.

**[276] Scherer, F. M., A. Beckenstein, E. Kaufer, and R. D. Murphy, *The Economics of Multi-Plant Operation.* Cambridge, Mass.: Harvard University Press, 1975.

**[277] Scherer, F. M., S. E. Herzstein, Jr., A. W. Dreyfoos, W. G. Whitney, O. J. Bachman, C. P. Pesek, C. J. Scott, T. G. Kelly and J. J. Galvin, *Patents and the Corporation.* 2d ed. Boston: James J. Galvin, 1959.

[278] Schmookler, J., "Bigness, Fewness, and Research," *Journal of Political Economy,* **67 (1959), 628–632.

[279] Schmookler, J., "Economic Sources of Inventive Activity," *Journal of Economic History,* **22** (1962), 1–20.

**[280] Schmookler, J., *Invention and Economic Growth.* Cambridge, Mass.: Harvard University Press, 1966.

*[281] Schumpeter, J. A., *The Theory of Economic Development,* translated by R. Opie. Cambridge, Mass.: Harvard University Press, 1934.

*[282] Schumpeter, J. A., *Business Cycles,* 2 vols. New York: McGraw-Hill, 1939.

*[283] Schumpeter, J. A., *Capitalism, Socialism, and Democracy.* New York: Harper, 1942.

*[284] Schumpeter, J. A., "The Creative Response in Economic History," *Journal of Economic History,* **7** (1947), 149–159. Reprinted in *Essays of J. A. Schumpeter,* ed. by R. V. Clemence. Cambridge, Mass.: Addison-Wesley, 1951.

*[285] Schumpeter, J. A., *History of Economic Analysis.* London: George Allen & Unwin, 1954.

**[286] Schwartzman, D., *Innovation in the Pharmaceutical Industry.* Baltimore: Johns Hopkins Press, 1976.

**[287] Scott, J. T., "Firm Versus Industry Variability in R & D Intensity," in *R & D, Patents, and Productivity,* ed. by Z. Griliches. Chicago: University of Chicago Press for the National Bureau of Economic Research, 1984.

[288] Shrieves, R. E., "Firm Size and Innovation: Further Evidence," *Industrial Organization Review,* **4** (1976), 26–33.

[289] Shrieves, R. E., "Market Structure and Innovation: A New Perspective," *Journal of Industrial Economics,* **26 (1978), 329–347.

**[290] Smith, B., "Technological Leadership in the Aluminum Industry," in *Technological Development and Economic Growth,* ed. by G. W. Wilson. Bloomington: Indiana University School of Business, 1971.

[291] Smyth, D. J., J. M. Samuels, and J. Tzoanos: "Patents, Profitability, Liquidity and Firm Size," *Applied Economics,* **4 (1972), 77–86.

[292] Soete, L. L. G., "Firm Size and Innovative Activity: The Evidence Reconsidered," *European Economic Review,* **12 (1979), 319–340.
[293] Solo, C., "Innovation in the Capitalist Process: A Critique of the Schumpeterian Theory," *Quarterly Journal of Economics,* **65** (1951), 417–428.
[294] Spence, A. M., "Cost Reduction, Competition, and Industry Performance," *Econometrica,* **52 (1984), 101–121.
[295] Stelzer, I. M., "Technical Progress and Market Structure," *Southern Economic Journal,* **23 (1956), 63–73.
[296] Stewart, M. B., "Noncooperative Oligopoly and Preemptive Innovation Without Winner-Take-All," *Quarterly Journal of Economics,* **98 (1983), 681–694.
**[297] Stigler, G. J., "Industrial Organization and Economic Progress," in *The State of the Social Sciences,* ed. by L. D. White. Chicago: University of Chicago Press, 1956.
[298] Sumrall, J. B., Jr., "Diffusion of the Basic Oxygen Furnace in the U.S. Steel Industry," *Journal of Industrial Economics,* **30 (1982), 421–447.
[299] Swan, P. L., "Market Structure and Technological Progress: The Influence of Monopoly on Product Innovation," *Quarterly Journal of Economics,* **84 (1970), 627–638.
[300] Swan, P. L., "The Influence of Monopoly on Product Innovation: Rejoinder," *Quarterly Journal of Economics,* **86 (1972), 346–349.
**[301] Tabbert, Jörg, *Unternehmensgrösse, Marktstruktur und technischer Fortschritt.* Göttingen: Vandenhoeck & Ruprecht, 1975.
[302] Tandon, P., "Rivalry and Excessive Allocation of Resources to Research," *Bell Journal of Economics,* **14 (1983), 152–165.
[303] Tandon, P., "Innovation, Market Structure, and Welfare," *American Economic Review,* **74 (1984), 394–403.
[304] Tarr, D. G., *On the Explanation of the Efficient Diffusion of Technology Across Nations.* Washington: U.S. Federal Trade Commission, 1980.
**[305] Teece, D. J., *The Multinational Corporation and the Resource Cost of International Technology Transfer.* Cambridge, Mass.: Ballinger, 1976.
[306] Teece, D. J., "Technology Transfer by Multinational Firms: The Resource Cost of Transferring Technological Know-How," *Economic Journal,* **87 (1977), 242–261.
**[307] Terleckyj, N. E., "R & D and U.S. Industrial Productivity in the 1970s," in *The Transfer and Utilization of Technical Knowledge,* ed. by D. Sahal. Lexington, Mass.: D. C. Heath, 1982.
[308] Teubal, M., "Threshold R & D Levels in Sectors of Advanced Technology," *European Economic Review,* **7** (1976), 395–402.
**[309] Teubal, M., "On User Needs and Need Determination: Aspects of the Theory of Technological Innovation," in *Industrial Innovation: Technology, Policy, Diffusion,* ed. by M. J. Baker. London: Macmillan, 1979.
[310] Teubal, M., "The R & D Performance through Time of Young, High-Technology Firms," *Research Policy,* **11 (1982), 333–346.
[311] Teubal, M. and P. Spiller, "Analysis of R & D Failure," *Research Policy,* **6** (1977), 255–275.
**[312] Tilton, J. E., *International Diffusion of Technology: The Case of Semiconductors.* Washington: Brookings, 1971.
[313] Uhlman, L., "Wie Viele Kleinere und Mittlere Unternehmen Betreiben Forschung und Entwicklung?" *Ifo-Schnelldienst,* **13/79 (1979), 7–13.
[314] U.S. Congress, Joint Economic Committee: *Special Study on Economic*

Change, 3, *Research and Innovation: Developing a Dynamic Nation.* Washington: U.S. Government Printing Office, 1980.

**[315] U.S. Federal Trade Commission, Bureau of Economics, *Statistical Report: Annual Line of Business Report, 1974, 1975, 1976, and 1977.* Washington: U.S. Government Printing Office, 1981, 1982, and 1985.

**[316] U.S. National Science Foundation, *Science and Engineering in American Industry.* Washington: U.S. Government Printing Office, 1956 and following years.

**[317] *United States* v. *Automobile Manufacturers' Association,* 307 F. Supp. 617 (1969).

**[318] Utterback, J. M., "The Dynamics of Product and Process Innovation," in *Technological Innovation for a Dynamic Economy,* ed. by C. T. Hill and J. M. Utterback. New York: Pergamon Press, 1979.

**[319] Vaughan, F. L., *The United States Patent System.* Norman: University of Oklahoma Press, 1956.

[320] Vernon, J. M. and P. Gusen, "Technical Change and Firm Size: The Pharmaceutical Industry," *Review of Economics and Statistics,* **56 (1974), 294–302.

[321] Vernon, R., "International Investment and International Trade in the Product Cycle," *Quarterly Journal of Economics,* **80 (1966), 190–207.

[322] Vernon, R., "The Product Cycle Hypothesis in a New International Environment," *Oxford Bulletin of Economics and Statistics,* **41 (1979), 255–267.

[323] Vickers, J., "Pre-emptive Patenting, Joint Ventures, and the Persistence of Oligopoly," *International Journal of Industrial Organization,* **3 (1985), 261–273.

[324] Villard, H., "Competition, Oligopoly and Research," *Journal of Political Economy,* **66** (1958), 483–497.

*[325] Von Weizsäcker, C. C., *Barriers to Entry: A Theoretical Treatment.* Berlin: Springer-Verlag, 1980.

[326] Waterson, M., "The Incentive to Invent When a New Input is Involved," *Economica,* **49 (1982), 435–445.

**[327] Webbink, D. W., *The Semiconductor Industry: A Survey of Structure, Conduct, and Performance.* Washington: U.S. Federal Trade Commission, 1977.

**[328] White, L. J., *The Automobile Industry Since 1945.* Cambridge, Mass.: Harvard University Press, 1971.

[329] White, L. J., "A Note on the Influence of Monopoly on Product Innovation," *Quarterly Journal of Economics,* **86 (1972), 342–345.

[330] Williams, B. R., ed., *Science and Technology in Economic Growth.* London: Macmillan, 1973.

[331] Williamson, O. E., "Innovation and Market Structure," *Journal of Political Economy,* **73 (1965), 67–73.

[332] Williamson, O. E., "Dominant Firms and the Monopoly Problem: Market Failure Considerations," *Harvard Law Review,* **85** (1972), 1512–1531.

[333] Williamson, O. E., "Predatory Pricing: A Strategic and Welfare Analysis," *Yale Law Journal,* **87** (1977), 284–340.

[334] Wilson, G. W., "Some Notes on the Economics of Diffusion," in *Technological Development and Economic Growth,* ed. by G. W. Wilson. Bloomington: Indiana University School of Business, 1971.

[335] Wilson, G. W., ed., *Technological Development and Economic Growth.* Bloomington: Indiana University School of Business, 1971.

[336] Wilson, R. W., "The Effect of Technological Environment and Product Rivalry on R & D Effort and Licensing of Inventions," *Review of Economics and Statistics*, **59** (1977), 171–178.
[337] Winter, S. G., "Satisficing, Selection, and the Innovating Remnant," *Quarterly Journal of Economics*, **85** (1971), 237–261.
[338] Winter, S. G., "Schumpeterian Competition in Alternative Technological Regimes," *Journal of Economic Behavior and Organization*, **5** (1984), 287–320.
[339] Worley, J. S., "Industrial Research and the New Competition," *Journal of Political Economy*, **69** (1961), 183–186.
[340] Yamey, B. S., "Monopoly, Competition and the Incentive to Invent: A Comment," *Journal of Law and Economics*, **13** (1970), 253–256.

INDEX